Kaplan Publishing are constantly finding new ... difference to your studies and our exciting onli... offer something different to students looking f...

This book comes with free MyKaplan online resources so that you can study anytime, anywhere. **This free online resource is not sold separately and is included in the price of the book.**

Having purchased this book, you have access to the following online study materials:

CONTENT	AAT	
	Text	Kit
Electronic version of the book	✓	✓
Progress tests with instant answers	✓	
Mock assessments online	✓	✓
Material updates	✓	✓

How to access your online resources

Kaplan Financial students will already have a MyKaplan account and these extra resources will be available to you online. You do not need to register again, as this process was completed when you enrolled. If you are having problems accessing online materials, please ask your course administrator.

If you are not studying with Kaplan and did not purchase your book via a Kaplan website, to unlock your extra online resources please go to www.mykaplan.co.uk/addabook (even if you have set up an account and registered books previously). You will then need to enter the ISBN number (on the title page and back cover) and the unique pass key number contained in the scratch panel below to gain access. You will also be required to enter additional information during this process to set up or confirm your account details.

If you purchased through the Kaplan Publishing website you will automatically receive an e-mail invitation to MyKaplan. Please register your details using this email to gain access to your content. If you do not receive the e-mail or book content, please contact Kaplan Publishing.

Your Code and Information

This code can only be used once for the registration of one book online. This registration and your online content will expire when the final sittings for the examinations covered by this book have taken place. Please allow one hour from the time you submit your book details for us to process your request.

Please scratch the film to access your unique code.

Please be aware that this code is case-sensitive and you will need to include the dashes within the passcode, but not when entering the ISBN.

KAPLAN PUBLISHING

AAT

AQ2016

PROFESSIONAL DIPLOMA IN ACCOUNTING

Synoptic Assessment 2020/21

FAMILIARISATION AND PRACTICE KIT – VEGGIE DELIGHTS LTD

This practice kit supports study for the following AAT qualifications:
AAT Professional Diploma in Accounting – Level 4
AAT Level 4 Diploma in Business Skills
AAT Professional Diploma in Accounting at SCQF – Level 8

KAPLAN
PUBLISHING

British Library Cataloguing-in-Publication Data

A catalogue record for this book is available from the British Library.

Published by:

Kaplan Publishing UK

Unit 2 The Business Centre

Molly Millar's Lane

Wokingham

Berkshire

RG41 2QZ

ISBN: 978-1-78740-812-8

Printed and bound in Great Britain.

CONTENTS

Live assessment pre-release material

This practice kit is based on the live assessment pre-release information for **Veggie Delights Ltd**. Make sure you download and print a copy from the AAT website to use in conjunction with this kit.

Studying this material will encourage you to think about the assessment topics in an integrated way, which is necessary for performing well in the synoptic assessment.

Note: Kaplan authors have invented scenarios and additional details when writing questions based on Veggie Delights Ltd. When sitting the live assessment, make sure you don't confuse what content is in the pre-release information and what additional details are in this practice kit.

You will find a wealth of other resources to help you with your studies on the AAT website:

www.aat.org.uk/

Quality and accuracy are of the utmost importance to us so if you spot an error in any of our products, please send an email to mykaplanreporting@kaplan.com with full details, or follow the link to the feedback form in MyKaplan.

Our Quality Co-ordinator will work with our technical team to verify the error and take action to ensure it is corrected in future editions.

SYNOPTIC ASSESSMENT

AAT AQ16 introduces a Synoptic Assessment, which students must complete if they are to achieve the appropriate qualification upon completion of a qualification. In the case of the Advanced Diploma in Accounting, students must pass all of the mandatory assessments and the Synoptic Assessment to achieve the qualification.

As a Synoptic Assessment is attempted following completion of individual units, it draws upon knowledge and understanding from those units. It may be appropriate for students to retain their study materials for individual units until they have successfully completed the Synoptic Assessment for that qualification.

Four units within the Professional Diploma in Accounting are mandatory. Of these, three are assessed individually in end of unit assessments, but this qualification also includes a synoptic assessment, sat towards the end of the qualification, which draws on and assesses knowledge and understanding from all four mandatory units:

- Financial statements of Limited Companies – end of unit assessment
- Management Accounting: Budgeting – end of unit assessment
- Management Accounting: Decision and Control – end of unit assessment
- Accounting Systems and Controls – assessed within the synoptic assessment only

Summary of learning outcomes from underlying units which are assessed in the synoptic assessment

Underlying unit	*Learning outcomes required*
Accounting Systems and Controls	LO1, LO2, LO3, LO4
Financial Statements of Limited Companies	LO1, LO5
Management Accounting: Budgeting	LO3
Management Accounting: Decision and Control	LO1, LO2, LO4, LO5

FORMAT OF THE ASSESSMENT

The specimen synoptic assessment comprises six tasks and covers all six assessment objectives. Students will be assessed by computer-based assessment. Marking of the assessment is partially by computer and partially human marked.

In any one assessment, students may not be assessed on all content, or on the full depth or breadth of a piece of content. The content assessed may change over time to ensure validity of assessment, but all assessment criteria will be tested over time.

The following weighting is based upon the AAT Qualification Specification documentation which may be subject to variation.

	Assessment objective	**Weighting**
AO1	Demonstrate an understanding of the roles and responsibilities of the accounting function within an organisation and examine ways of preventing and detecting fraud and systemic weaknesses.	20%
AO2	Evaluate budgetary reporting; its effectiveness in controlling and improving organisational performance.	15%
AO3	Evaluate an organisation's accounting control systems and procedures.	15%
AO4	Analyse an organisation's decision making and control using management accounting tools.	15%
AO5	Analyse an organisation's decision making and control using ratio analysis.	20%
AO6	Analyse the internal controls of an organisation and make recommendations.	15%
	Total	100%

Time allowed: 3 hours

PASS MARK: The pass mark for all AAT assessments is 70%.

Always keep your eye on the clock and make sure you attempt all questions!

The detailed syllabus and study guide written by the AAT can be found at:

www.aat.org.uk/

INDEX TO QUESTIONS AND ANSWERS

EXAM TECHNIQUE

- **Do not skip any of the material** in the syllabus.
- In particular, make sure you are comfortable with **assumed knowledge** from other papers at this level and those from lower levels.
- Make sure you are **familiar** with the live assessment pre-release information and have read through it at least twice.
- **Read each question** *very* carefully.
- **Double-check your answer** before committing yourself to it.
- Answer **every** question – if you do not know an answer to a multiple choice question or true/false question, you don't lose anything by guessing. Think carefully before you **guess.**
- If you are answering a multiple-choice question, **eliminate first those answers that you know are wrong.** Then choose the most appropriate answer from those that are left.
- **Don't panic** if you realise you've answered a question incorrectly. Getting one question wrong will not mean the difference between passing and failing.

Computer-based exams – tips

- Do not attempt a CBA until you have **completed all study material** relating to it.
- On the AAT website there is a CBA demonstration. It is **ESSENTIAL** that you attempt this before your real CBA. You will become familiar with how to move around the CBA screens and the way that questions are formatted, increasing your confidence and speed in the actual exam.
- Be sure you understand how to use the **software** before you start the exam. If in doubt, ask the assessment centre staff to explain it to you.
- Questions are **displayed on the screen** and answers are entered using keyboard and mouse. At the end of the exam, in the case of those units not subject to human marking, you are given a certificate showing the result you have achieved.
- In addition to the traditional multiple-choice question type, CBAs will also contain **other types of questions**, such as number entry questions, drag and drop, true/false, pick lists or drop down menus or hybrids of these.
- In some CBAs you will have to type in complete computations or written answers.
- You need to be sure you **know how to answer questions** of this type before you sit the exam, through practice.

KAPLAN'S RECOMMENDED REVISION APPROACH

QUESTION PRACTICE IS THE KEY TO SUCCESS

Success in professional examinations relies upon you acquiring a firm grasp of the required knowledge at the tuition phase. In order to be able to do the questions, knowledge is essential.

However, the difference between success and failure often hinges on your exam technique on the day and making the most of the revision phase of your studies.

The **Kaplan Study Text** is the starting point, designed to provide the underpinning knowledge to tackle all questions. However, in the revision phase, poring over text books is not the answer.

Kaplan Pocket Notes are designed to help you quickly revise a topic area; however you then need to practise questions. There is a need to progress to exam style questions as soon as possible, and to tie your exam technique and technical knowledge together.

The importance of question practice cannot be over-emphasised.

The recommended approach below is designed by expert tutors in the field, in conjunction with their knowledge of the examiner and the specimen assessment.

You need to practise as many questions as possible in the time you have left.

OUR AIM

Our aim is to get you to the stage where you can attempt exam questions confidently, to time, in a closed book environment, with no supplementary help (i.e. to simulate the real examination experience).

Practising your exam technique is also vitally important for you to assess your progress and identify areas of weakness that may need more attention in the final run up to the examination.

In order to achieve this we recognise that initially you may feel the need to practice some questions with open book help.

Good exam technique is vital.

THE KAPLAN REVISION PLAN

Stage 1: Assess areas of strengths and weaknesses

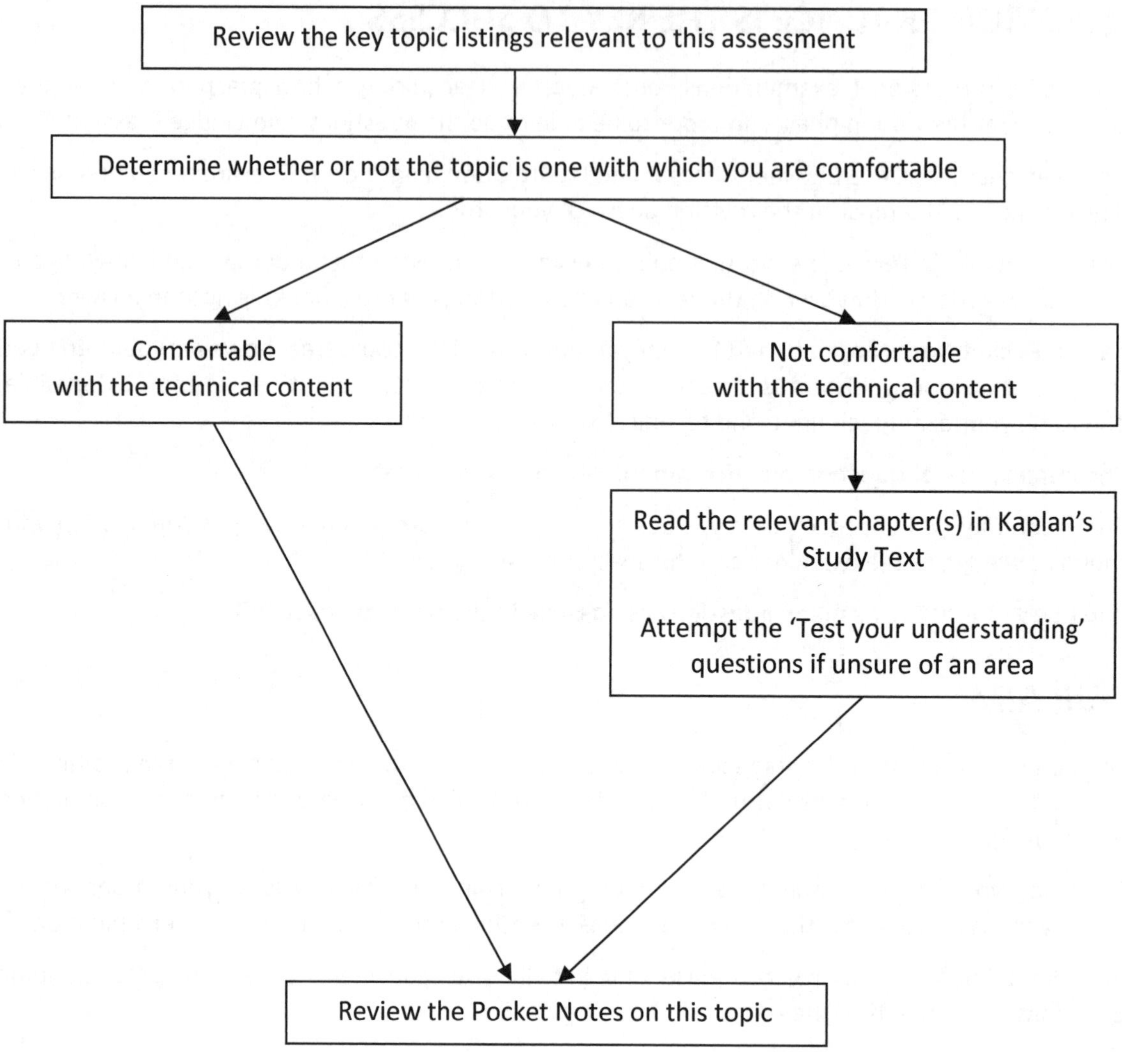

Stage 2: Familiarisation and practice questions

Follow the order of revision of topics as presented in this practice kit and attempt the questions in the order suggested.

Try to avoid referring to Study Texts and your notes and the model answer until you have completed your attempt.

Review your attempt with the model answer and assess how much of the answer you achieved.

Comfortable with question attempt → Only revisit when comfortable with questions on all topic areas

Not comfortable with question attempts → Focus on these areas by:

- Reworking 'Test your understanding' questions in Kaplan's Study Text
- Revisiting the technical content from Kaplan's Pocket Notes
- Working any remaining questions on that area in this practice kit

Stage 3: Final pre-exam revision

We recommend that you **attempt at least one mock examination** containing a set of previously unseen exam-standard questions based on the live assessment pre-release information.

Attempt the mock CBA online in timed, closed book conditions to simulate the real exam experience.

Also ensure that you have worked through the two sample assessments carefully and thought how to answer the same questions from the perspective of the company in the live pre-seen release.

Section 1

COMMENTARY ON LIVE PRE-RELEASE INFORMATION

1 ADVANCED PRE-RELEASE INFORMATION

INSTRUCTIONS TO CANDIDATES

This material is designed to contextualise the tasks you will receive in your live assessments.

This document has been made available to you ahead of your assessment. Studying this material will encourage you to think about the assessment topics in an integrated way, which is necessary for performing well in the synoptic assessment.

You will not be able to take a copy of this document into the assessment with you. However, you will have access to this material through pop-up windows in the assessment.

VEGGIE DELIGHTS LTD

COMPANY BACKGROUND AND PERFORMANCE TO DATE

Veggie Delights Ltd is a private limited company, based in Bournemouth, which operates a small chain of vegetarian restaurants across the south of England. Its approach is to only use locally sourced, organic produce in their meals.

The business was started 15 years ago by Sean O'Keefe and Caroline Rowley when they opened a restaurant in Christchurch, a small town near Bournemouth. Although the early years of the business were quite difficult, the trend towards eating healthy and additive free foods has boosted the popularity of organic foods. This has resulted in a dramatic rise in both sales and profits over the last four years.

This surge in popularity and significantly improved operational performance has led to a further five restaurants opening across the south of England in the last three years. The intention is to open another four restaurants in the next financial year.

From the beginning, Veggie Delights Ltd has always been focused on providing a wide range of healthy children's meals in addition to its main menu. This has proved to be an important part of the success of the business, with families being a large proportion of its restaurant customers.

Last year, Veggie Delights Ltd decided to expand its food offering by allowing customers to order meals online. The meals can then be either collected from the restaurant or, for a small additional charge, be delivered directly to the customer. Due to logistical issues with deliveries, this service is currently only available from two of the restaurants for customers who live within a one-mile radius of these restaurants. Although the option to order meals for delivery has proved to be popular at these two restaurants, there has been a 5% reduction in the number of customers eating in the two restaurants since the service was introduced.

In order to facilitate the online ordering service, Veggie Delights Ltd commissioned designers to create a bespoke website. Due to the large number of variations that are available for each meal, creating the e-commerce element of the website has proved difficult. The total cost to date of the website has been £45,000, well over the original estimate of £25,000.

Despite the large amount of money already spent on the website, it has proved to be very unreliable and since its launch has had down time amounting to 15% of total time.

The expansion of Veggie Delights Ltd into multiple restaurants has meant that additional staff have had to be recruited to manage this increased operational activity. Veggie Delights Ltd has also had to rent premises in Bournemouth to act as the business's head office.

STRATEGIC PLAN

Veggie Delights Ltd has a strategic plan which looks to consider its business environment for the next five years. Each year the plan is updated based on the previous 12 months' trading. Extracts from the most recent strategic plan are provided below.

STRATEGIC PLAN EXTRACTS

Business Development

For the business to continue to grow at the rates achieved over the last three years, it is vital that new products are developed and that customers continue to be given the choice to eat in or have food delivered. In addition, the business should look to secure its own supply of fresh produce and exploit the opportunities that can arise from this.

1. Eat-in restaurants

Veggie Delights Ltd needs to continue to be at the front of new developments in the food market. The business should look to expand its product offering by:

- Creating a standalone vegan menu
- Only stocking drinks that are organically certified

2. Online Service

All restaurants within the chain should have an online ordering capability and the availability of online delivery should be extended to a five-mile radius of each restaurant. Further financial resources need to be given to the website development to make sure that its reliability is improved to acceptable levels.

3. Organic Farm

In addition to the expansion of the restaurant business, the medium-term strategy should be to move into the growing of produce, in organically certified farms, that can then be supplied directly to the restaurants. Subject to the success of the farms, the longer-term aim is to diversify the business by growing enough produce to supply supermarkets.

Risk

The rapid expansion of the business over the last few years has led to an increased risk profile for Veggie Delights Ltd. It is vital that these risks are recognised and managed.

1. Competition

The increase in popularity of heathy eating has brought a number of new competitors into the market. This may have an impact on future profitability.

2. Overheads

The growth of the business has resulted in a dramatic increase in the level of overheads. This is partly due to the new head office, additional head office staff and a regional management team. There have also been increases in the level of business rates, further increasing operating overheads.

3. Controls

The expansion of the business requires strong internal controls to be in place. Although the business has invested in additional experienced staff to manage the growth, attention must be paid to installing and monitoring controls to make sure they are fit for purpose.

Brand Awareness

In order to maintain growth levels and increase customer loyalty, a wide-ranging social media campaign to put the Veggie Delights Ltd brand in front of new and existing customers is required. The campaign will focus on promoting three areas:

1. Awards and recognition

The business has won several awards for its innovation and creativity in the organic vegetarian food sector. Moving forwards, the business must ensure maximum exposure for any industry recognition it receives.

2. Merchandising

In order to maximise the benefit of the family friendly reputation of the business, a range of merchandise needs to be developed. The goods will consist of a range of toys made from sustainable materials. The toys will be based on the vegetables that are contained within the children's menu.

3. Introduction of a loyalty card

To encourage customers to choose to eat more regularly at the restaurants, a loyalty card will be introduced that will reward customers with discounted meals and drinks and other seasonal offers.

Sustainability

The business has always prided itself on being a good employer, supporting local suppliers and minimising its environmental impact. As the business grows, the challenge is to make sure those principles stay embedded within the business.

1. Zero waste philosophy

The business will continue to strive towards having no food waste within its meal production processes. Any food waste that arises from either the business or its customers will be composted and delivered to suppliers for their use in growing produce.

2. Staff pay

A minimum hourly rate of £10.50 per hour will be introduced for all staff. This rate will be constantly reviewed and kept ahead of the national minimum wage.

3. Compostable cardboard trays

The business will remove the use of re-usable china plates from restaurants and replace these with cardboard trays which can then be utilised within the composting process.

Organisational Structure

The business has, until now, only used cash generated from operations to fund expansion. It is recognised that the business may have to look at alternative operating models if it is to achieve its ambitious growth targets.

1. Venture capital

The sale of an equity stake in the business to a venture capital organisation may be necessary to provide sufficient funds.

2. Franchise

The opening of further restaurants in the future could be on a franchise basis which would help to ease pressure on cash flow, and potentially speed up growth.

STAFF

Some of Veggie Delights Ltd key personnel are listed below:

Managing Director	Sean O'Keefe
Deputy Managing Director	Caroline Rowley
Finance Director	Agnes Copeland
Human Resources Director	Lauren Bristow
Regional Operations Manager	Sergey Dashdamirov
Commercial Manager	Conor Seddon
Financial Controller	Amar Hameer
Purchasing Manager	Lokesh Ashtari
Development Chef	Nina Proctor
Accounts Payable Manager	Aida Marks
Accounts Payable Clerk	Supul Khayyam
General Accounts Clerk	Maisie Holmes
Cashier	Tommy Mills
Payroll Manager	Nelson Badar

VEGGIE DELIGHTS LTD'S FINANCIAL STATEMENTS

Veggie Delights Ltd – Statement of profit or loss for the year ended 31 December 20X9

	£
Revenue	4,189,380
Cost of sales	(2,146,134)
Gross profit	2,043,246
Operating expenses	(1,716,499)
Profit from operations	326,747
Finance costs	(1,809)
Profit before tax	324,938
Tax	(61,738)
Profit for the period from continuing operations	**263,200**

Veggie Delights Ltd – Statement of financial position as at 31 December 20X9

	£
ASSETS	
Non-current assets	
Property, plant and equipment	207,184
Intangible assets	45,000
Current assets	
Inventories	36,947
Trade receivables	1,073
Cash and cash equivalents	354,888
	392,908
Total assets	**645,092**
EQUITY AND LIABILITIES	
Equity	
Ordinary share capital (£1 shares)	1,000
Retained earnings	269,443
Total equity	270,443
Non-current liabilities	
Bank loan	9,675
Current liabilities	
Trade payables	303,236
Tax liabilities	61,738
	364,974
Total liabilities	374,649
Total equity and liabilities	**645,092**

2 ANALYSIS AND COMMENTARY

A key question is how best to assess the pre-release information.

The simplest approach is to read through each section and ask yourself what this is telling you about the company, focussing on control issues and the effectiveness of its systems and processes.

Let us take each section in turn:

COMPANY BACKGROUND AND PERFORMANCE TO DATE

- Veggie Delights Ltd ("Veggie Delights") operates five vegetarian restaurants. As such controls relating to cash receipts and managing tills are particularly important as there could be a high risk of fraud. Furthermore, controls linked to quality are also critical, whether the sourcing and purchase of local ingredients or those linked to food preparation.
- The company has expanded rapidly which, while encouraging as far as profit is concerned, raises many issues for control systems – are systems that worked when the company was smaller still effective now, is there a need for greater segregation of duties, do some controls need to be more formalised, are some functions too large for effective management without restructuring and/or is it now easier for frauds to get lost in the overall volume of business?
- The importance of having a good children's menu (and the trade that brings) should be reflected by a system of key performance indicators (KPIs) that allow the relative performance of adult and children's meals to be monitored and controlled. For example, do both have the same mark up or are children's meal priced relatively lower to attract families?
- Similarly there need to be controls and performance measures to allow the owners to monitor the success and viability of home delivery, especially as they seem to displace restaurant customers.
- Attempts at e-commerce means that adequate IT and website controls are essential, whether to prevent hacking and loss of customer data, or to ensure that prices and menus are kept up to date so customer orders can be processed quickly and accurately. The over spend on website development is concerning – does this reflect a lack of adequate authorisation controls over capital spending? Likewise, does the company have a scorecard to assess website performance and take action if required?
- The ongoing rise in workforce numbers increases the risk of new recruits not being set up correctly on payroll, of controls over overtime and expenses being inadequate and staff being paid too much / too little.

STRATEGIC PLAN

The strategic plan is updated every year. If this also means that budgets are only adjusted annually, then there is a high risk that they will become out of date, limiting their effectiveness as a control mechanism.

Business development

- Menu choices – with vegan options, controls over food preparation are vital to avoid contamination and the company will need separate KPIs to monitor and control performance of each line.
- Online service – key risks are (1) choice of delivery system – should they use third party couriers or do it in-house? (2) Impact on number of customers coming to the restaurant

  [Note: A circle with a radius of 5 miles has 25× the area of a circle with radius 1 mile and the company's experience of the latter was that it displaced 5% of restaurant customers. How many would be lost under the new plan? Would it even be worth still running restaurants or should they switch to a purely home delivery model?]
- Organic farming – key risks are (1) Capital investment required will be high (2) It would require a completely new and different skill set (3) It would change ingredient costs from being mainly variable in nature to having a significant fixed element, increasing risks.

Risk

- Competition – to help manage the risk from new rivals, the company needs to set up and monitor suitable, benchmarked, KPIs looking at relative margins, market share, prices, etc.
- Overheads – the company has identified a need to control OH. This could involve better controls over authorisation of purchases, recruitment of new staff as well as better decision making over the opening of new restaurants.

Brand awareness

- Awards – as well as ensuring the message is put on the website or social media, the company should monitor whether this is working – for example, by using questionnaires to assess brand recognition.
- Merchandising – decisions will need to be made as to which products to make, how to make them and how to price them – all involving MDCL topics in task 4.
- Loyalty cards – the decision whether to adopt these should be considered using relevant cash flows (e.g. comparing sales gained vs contribution lost through discounts). If adopted then the impact would need to be incorporated into budgeting and KPIs to monitor their effectiveness.

Sustainability

In the real assessment you may have to evaluate how well the company is doing in terms of operating in a sustainable manner. Using the environmental/social/economic categories we can see that Veggie Delights is making advances in all three areas:

- Environmental - Veggie Delights is trying to reduce landfill and has a low carbon footprint due to local sourcing of ingredients.
- Social – Veggie Delights uses local suppliers and seeks to pay fair wages to staff.
- Economic – Veggie Delights does seem to be investing for the future but must be wary of trying to grow too quickly and risk over-trading.

Furthermore, any threats to the company's sustainability credentials could have a damaging impact on its brand and reputation, so it is vital that suitable controls are in place and working effectively, such as screening potential suppliers before placing orders.

Organisational structure

- Venture capital – potential investors would be very interested in Veggie Delights' financial statements and task 5 (ratios) could take this perspective.
- Franchising – most franchising agreements would involve the franchisee paying the franchisor (Veggie Delights) a percentage of either revenue or profits. Given this, Veggie Delights would need controls in place to reassure it that figures quoted by the franchisee are accurate and reasonable and that they are not being defrauded.

  In addition there is the risk that poor quality control by a franchisee could damage Veggie Delights' brand name, again indicating the need for suitable controls, such as training, insistence that the franchisee only uses preferred suppliers, etc.

STAFF

A list of key staff help you see how the organisation is structured and also if there are obvious control issues relating to responsibilities – for example, not having a separate Accounts Payable Clerk and Accounts Receivable Clerk may result in problems with segregation of duties.

VEGGIE DELIGHTS' FINANCIAL STATEMENTS

You could calculate ratios to see if any key problems are highlighted:

	(Working)	**Ratio**
Gross margin (%)	2,043,246/4,189,380	48.8%
Operating margin (%)	326,747/4,189,380	7.8%
ROCE (%)	326,747/(9,675 + 270,443)	116.6%
Current ratio	392,908/364,974	1.08:1
Quick ratio	(1,073+354,888)/ 364,974	0.98:1
Inventory days	(36,947/2,146,134) × 365	6 days
Receivables days	(1,073/4,189,380) × 365	0.1 days
Payables days	(303,236/2,146,134) × 365	52 days
Operating cycle	6 + 0 - 52	(56) days
Gearing (Debt/Equity)	9,675/270,443	0.04:1
Gearing (debt/total long term finance)	9,675/(9,675 + 270,443)	3.5%

The effectiveness of such an exercise is limited by the fact that we only have one year of results and no industry averages, so have no basis of comparison to evaluate figures.

Furthermore, interpreting the figures is made more difficult due to the high growth experienced by the company. This means that year end balances are likely to be higher than was typical throughout the period.

Given all this, we can make the following comments:

- Gross margin is good, indicating that the model of locally-sourced, vegetarian food is working.
- However, the operating profit margin seem low, possibly indicating a need to review areas such as business rents and rates, and administration to see if there are cost inefficiencies or control issues.
- Overall, ROCE is exceptionally high but this is perhaps more representative of a very low capital employed than high profit. The low value of equity in particular is due to low retained profits, indicating that profitability before 20X9 was much lower.
- It could be argued that there is no real concerns over short term liquidity risk as (a) the company has high cash reserves and (b) the operating cycle is negative, indicating that cash is received before payments must be made to suppliers. However, both current and quick ratios are low.
- Inventory days at 6 days are as expected, being a mixture of fresh goods and some longer life items such as spices. It is vital that the shop mangers keep an eye on 'use by' dates to reduce throwing food away and/or compromising the quality of meals served
- We are not told what trade receivables relate to - presumably most customers will pay immediately whether in restaurants or via the website. Receivables might relate to
    - o Invoicing suppliers for food waste recycled for composting (if they actually charge for this).
    - o Charging firms to advertise on Veggie Delight's website.
    - o Some local businesses who use a restaurant on a regular basis may have been allowed to set up an account and are invoiced at the end of the month.

  However, without a split between cash sales and credit sales, the calculated receivables days figure is difficult to interpret.
- Payables days seem high, although this could be unrepresentative due to high growth. However, is there a danger that we are at risk of upsetting suppliers, which could result in delays in delivery or poor quality, both of which could seriously compromise Veggie Delights' quality and ability to meet customer orders?
- Financial gearing is low, so there should be scope to raise debt finance for new restaurants / buying farms / etc if required.

WHAT NEXT?

You do not need to learn any of the above analysis – the aim is to help you feel comfortable with the company and what it does and to think about the assessment topics in an integrated way.

In some respects the main reason for looking at the pre-release material is to feel comfortable with the scenario and to know what is there so you can refer back to it if necessary.

- In sample assessment 1 all relevant information was given to you within the tasks, so there was little need to refer back to the pre-release material in order to answer them.
- However, in sample assessment 2 you needed to refer back to the financial statements in order to calculate ratios.

Section 2

PRACTICE QUESTIONS

TASK 1.1

Assessment objective 1	Demonstrate an understanding of the roles and responsibilities of the accounting function within an organisation and examine ways of preventing and detecting fraud and systemic weaknesses.

1 STATUTORY DUTY

Who has the statutory duty to prepare accounts for Veggie Delights?

The company auditors.	
The directors of the company.	
Finance Director.	
Financial Controller.	
Companies House.	

2 RESPONSIBILITY

Who is responsible for maintaining sound risk management and internal control systems within Veggie Delights?

The company auditors.	
The directors of the company.	
Finance Director.	
Financial Controller.	
Companies House.	

3 BANK RECONCILIATION 1

You are assisting with the month-end bank reconciliation at Veggie Delights.

The bank statement has been compared with the cash book and the following differences identified:

1. Cheques totalling £1,629 paid into the bank at the end of the month are not showing on the bank statement.
2. Bank interest paid of £106 was not entered in the cash book.
3. A cheque for £350 written on 2 January has been incorrectly entered in the cash book at 2 December.
4. Receipts from website customers of £1,645 had cleared the bank but has not been entered in the cash book.

The balance showing on the bank statement at 31 December is a credit of £363 and the balance in the cash book is a debit of £103.

Use the following table to show the THREE adjustments you need to make to the cash book.

Adjustment	*Amount* £	*Debit/Credit*

4 BANK RECONCILIATION 2

Which of the following errors would be picked up by a bank reconciliation? (Select all that apply)

	Yes	No
A trade customer was accidentally invoiced twice for the same item.		
A trade customer took a 2% prompt payment discount despite not having paid within the timescales required to earn a discount.		
Bank interest received had not been posted to the cash book.		
A payment to a supplier of £2,500 had accidentally been posted as £250.		

5 SALES LEDGER CONTROL ACCOUNT RECONCILIATION 1

[Note: Veggie Delights appears to have very few credit sales but it is still worth revising the principles of reconciliations]

You are working on the final accounts of a company that operates a manual accounting system.

You have the following information:

(a) A casting error has been made and one of the customer accounts has been undercast by £65.

(b) Sales returns totalling £280 have not been entered in a customer's individual ledger.

(c) A receipt of £1,300 from a customer has been credited to the customer's account in the sales ledger as 130.

(d) A credit sale of £3,000 (excluding VAT at 20%) has not been included in the relevant customer's account in the sales ledger.

(e) A customer account with a balance of £99 has been duplicated in the list of balances.

(f) A customer with a credit balance of £50 has been listed as a debit balance of £50.

You now need to make the appropriate adjustments in the table below.

For each adjustment clearly state the amount and whether the item should be added or subtracted from the list of balances. If no adjustment is required enter '0' into the amount column.

	Add/Subtract	£
Total from list of balances		1,100
Adjustment for (a)		
Adjustment for (b)		
Adjustment for (c)		
Adjustment for (d)		
Adjustment for (e)		
Adjustment for (f)		
Revised total to agree with SLCA		3,116

6 SALES LEDGER CONTROL ACCOUNT RECONCILIATION 2

Which of the following errors would be picked up by performing a sales ledger control account reconciliation?

	Yes	No
A trade customer was accidentally invoiced twice for the same item.		
A trade customer was sold items at the wrong price.		
Credit balances had been omitted from the list of receivables balances.		
A payment from a customer of £230 had accidentally been posted as £320 to their individual account in the receivables ledger.		

7 PURCHASES LEDGER CONTROL ACCOUNT RECONCILIATION

You are working on the final accounts of Veggie Delights, which operates a manual accounting system.

You have the following information:

(a) A payment of £1,277 to a supplier has been debited to the supplier's account in the purchases ledger as £1,722.

(b) A supplier with a debit balance of £2,170 has been listed as a credit balance.

(c) A credit purchase return of £1,000 (net of VAT at 20%) has not been included in the relevant supplier's account in the purchase ledger.

(d) A casting error has been made and one of the supplier accounts has been overcast by £132.

(e) A supplier account with a balance of £2,100 has been omitted from the list.

(f) A credit purchase has been entered into the individual account net of VAT at 20%. The net amount is £600.

You now need to make the appropriate adjustments in the table below. For each adjustment clearly state the amount and whether the item should be added or subtracted from the list of balances.

	Add/Subtract	£
Total from list of balances		132,589
Adjustment for (a)		
Adjustment for (b)		
Adjustment for (c)		
Adjustment for (d)		
Adjustment for (e)		
Adjustment for (f)		
Revised total to agree with PLCA		129,582

8 ERRORS

You are working on the accounting records of Veggie Delights.

A trial balance has been drawn up and a suspense account opened. You need to make some corrections and adjustments for the year ended 31 December 20Y0.

You may ignore VAT in this task.

Record the journal entries needed in the general ledger to deal with the items below.

(a) Motor expenses of £4,500 have been posted to the Motor Vehicles at Cost account in error. The other side of the entry is correct.

Journal

	Dr £	*Cr* £

(b) Office sundries costing £16 were paid for by cash. Only the entry to the cash account was made.

Journal

	Dr £	*Cr* £

(c) No entries have been made for closing inventory as at 31 December 20Y0. It has been valued at a selling price of £50,400. The sales price has had 20% added onto its original cost.

Journal

	Dr £	*Cr* £

(d) Discounts allowed of £1,270 have been posted as £1,720 on both sides of the entry.

Journal

	Dr £	*Cr* £

9 CHANGEOVER

The Board of Veggie Delights are considering updating the accounting system.

Agnes Copeland (FD) is suggesting that the direct changeover method be adopted. However, Sean O'Keefe (Managing Director) has argued that direct changeover is usually the highest risk alternative available.

Which TWO of the following controls can mitigate the risk of system failure during direct changeover?

Testing	
Training	
System documentation	
Data backup	
Check digits	

10 INFORMATION SYSTEM CONTROLS

Information system controls can be classified as 'security controls' and 'integrity controls'.

Drag and drop the following controls into the correct category.

	Security	Integrity
Locked doors		
Passwords		
Batch totals		
Reconciliation		
CCTV		
Check digits		
Authorisation of data entry		
Fire alarms		

11 PURCHASE CYCLE CONTROLS 1

Veggie Delights has experienced occasions when payment was made for goods not received.

Which TWO of the following controls in a purchase cycle could be implemented to reduce the risk of payment of goods not received?

Sequentially pre-numbered purchase requisitions and sequence check.	
Matching of goods received note with purchase invoice.	
Goods are inspected for condition and quantity and agreed to purchase order before acceptance.	
Daily update of inventory system.	

12 PURCHASE CYCLE CONTROLS 2

Veggie Delights has experienced occasions when unnecessary goods and services were purchased.

Which TWO of the following controls in the purchase cycle could be implemented to reduce the risk of procurement of unnecessary goods and services?

Centralised purchasing department.	
Sequentially pre-numbered purchase requisitions and sequence check.	
Orders can only be placed with suppliers from the approved suppliers list.	
All purchase requisitions are signed as authorised by an appropriate manager.	

13 EXPENSE CLAIM CONTROLS

Harry Grisham has been appointed as the new IT manager at Veggie Delights. Harry really enjoys the job and even though the remuneration is not great, the other managers at the company have explained the way they 'get around' that issue. The sales manager explains to Harry that the key is to 'put everything on expenses – private petrol, drinks and even clothing. It's all fine and as long as you have a receipt, no-one in the finance department will question it'. He continues that 'It's fine because the board are aware of it and turn a blind eye'.

Which ONE of the following essential internal control measures is evidently missing?

Veggie Delights lacks a control environment as the board are not setting an ethical tone at the top.	
Veggie Delights lacks an Internal Audit department.	
Veggie Delights lacks an experienced finance manager.	
Veggie Delights lacks an external auditor.	

14 PASSWORDS 1

You have been asked to set up a password for Veggie Delights' accounting system.

Which of the following would be the most secure?

24june1963	
LaraJo	
mypassword	
Qwerty123!#	

15 PASSWORDS 2

You have been asked to set up a new system of passwords for Veggie Delights' accounting system.

Which TWO of the following would reduce the effectiveness of passwords?

Requirement that passwords are changed every two weeks	
Users are allowed to choose their own passwords	
Automatic lock-out after 3 failed attempts to access system	
Making the sharing of passwords a disciplinary offence	
Displaying the password on the screen when entered	

16 INTERNAL CONTROLS 1

An internal control system in an organisation consists of five components: the control environment, the risk assessment process, the information system, control activities and monitoring of controls.

Match each of the following activities to the component that it illustrates.

	Control environment	Information system	Control activities
The process of preparing the financial statements			
Locking the inventory storeroom			

17 INTERNAL CONTROLS 2

Veggie Delights is looking at introducing new internal controls to help reduce the risk of fraud.

Match each of the following activities to the type of control that it illustrates.

	Authorisation	Information processing	Physical control
The financial controller will count petty cash on a weekly basis			
There will be two keys to a locked safe: one held by the FD and the other by the MD.			

18 INTERNAL CONTROLS 3

Veggie Delights is looking at introducing new computer controls to reduce payroll fraud. Computer controls can be described as "general" and "application".

Match each of the following activities to the type of computer control that it illustrates.

	General	Application
Storing extra copies of programs and data files off-site		
New programmes to check data fields on input transactions		
Manual checks to ensure that input data were authorised		
Password protection limiting access to data		
Range checks on payroll processing		
Manual checks to ensure that timesheets are authorised before details are processed		

19 INTERNAL CONTROLS 4

Veggie Delights is looking at introducing new internal controls but the directors are concerned that even the best controls still have limitations.

Indicate whether the following limitations are true or false.

	True	False
The cost of implementing controls may be more expensive than the benefits gained due to reduced risk		
The effectiveness of many controls rely on the integrity of those applying them		
Internal controls are only applied to material items so smaller items remain unchecked		
Standard controls may not be designed to deal with unusual transactions		

20 FRAUD 1

Sean O'Keefe is concerned that some Veggie Delights restaurant staff may be misappropriating customer remittances.

Which TWO of the following control activities would best reduce the risk of this fraud occurring?

Segregation of duties between cash payments and recording at head office	
Post opening by two people	
Daily reconciliation of recorded till sales and cash taken within restaurants	
Regular banking of cash and cheques received in restaurants	

21 FRAUD 2

The financial controller is worried that fictitious employees could be included on the payroll by a dishonest employee from the accounts department.

Which ONE of the following control activities would best prevent this occurring?

Payroll standing data periodically printed out and checked on a line-by-line basis to independently held employee details	
Use of hierarchical passwords over standing data files	
Pre-authorisation of all amendments to payroll standing data by an independent official	
Supervision of the wages pay out by an independent official	

TASK 1.2

Assessment objective 2	Evaluate budgetary reporting; its effectiveness in controlling and improving organisational performance.

22 TRAINING COSTS

Staff training within Veggie Delights has lacked focus but to facilitate future expansion, the directors of Veggie Delights want formalised training schemes in place on topics such as food hygiene and customer service. Given this, they have appointed a new training manager, Petr Higgs.

One month later, Petr received the following email from Lauren Bristow (HR Director)

To: Petr Higgs, Training Manager

From: Lauren Bristow

Subject: Costs out of control

I am writing to express concern over the results of your first month in charge of training.

In particular you need to explain the reasons for your cost overrun:

	Budget	**Actual**
Number of trainees	20	25
Fixed costs (£)	13,000	12,900
Variable costs (£)	1,000	1,200
Total cost (£)	14,000	14,100

Adverse variance £100

Please come and see me immediately.

Petr was alarmed by the email as he didn't even know there was going to be a performance appraisal of this kind and certainly hadn't been involved in any budgeting or target setting.

He was also concerned that there seemed to be no mention of how good the training was.

(a) BRIEFLY discuss THREE weaknesses in the above use of performance reports to improve the focus of training within Veggie Delights. (9 marks)

Weakness 1

Weakness 2

Weakness 3

(b) **Outline THREE performance indicators that could be used to assess the quality of the training provided.** **(6 marks)**

Performance Indicator 1

Performance Indicator 2

Performance Indicator 3

(Total 15 marks)

23 BUDGETING

Sergey Dashdamirov (Regional Operations Manager) has presented a budget proposal for 20Y0 for approval by the Board of Veggie Delights. Amar Hameer (Financial Controller) has already completed some analysis of the budget but is currently ill, so you have been asked to comment on the proposal.

Budget:

	Actual 20X9	**Budget 20Y0**	**% change**
	£000	£000	
Sales revenue	4,189	5,027	20.0%
Cost of sales	(2,146)	(2,511)	17.0%
Gross profit	**2,043**	**2,516**	
Operating expenses	(1,716)	(1,694)	(1.3%)
Operating profit	**327**	**822**	

Analysis:

	Actual 20X9	**Budget 20Y0**	**% change**
Number of restaurants	6	10	66.7%
Sales volume (000s of customers)	209	261	25.0%
Average revenue per customer	£20.04	£19.26	(3.9%)
Gross profit margin	48.8%	50.0%	

Notes:

- Veggie Delights won an industry award for 'Most innovative vegetarian menus" in December 20X9.
- Latest market forecasts for 20Y0 show a 10% growth in demand for vegetarian meals and a 15% growth in demand for vegan meals.
- Furthermore, it is expected that 80% of restaurants will have vegan options on their menus by the end of 20Y0, compared to 70% in 20X9.

Evaluate the budget for 20Y0 by discussing the following assumed (or implied) growth rates and margins. In your answer discuss whether or not you feel the figures are realistic and why. (15 marks)

Figure	Whether or not realistic	Marks
Sales volume growth of 25.0%		4
Sales revenue growth of 20.0%		3
Cost of sales growth of 17.0%		3
Fall in operating expenses of 1.3%		3

Conclusion – whether or not the budget is realistic (2 marks)

24 VEGGIE DELIGHTS' BUDGETING PROCESS

Veggie Delights is about to undertake the next annual budgeting cycle. The different managers involved have been provided with guidance notes to help them with this.

Veggie Delights Budgeting Guidance (extracts)

Inflation:

Inflation should be allowed for when appropriate. For wages, rent costs and food costs inflation, restaurant managers can select between the RPI (retail price index) and the CPI (consumer price index which excludes mortgage payments). Both these indexes measure past inflation in the United Kingdom where Veggie Delights is based.

No guidance is given about inflation of other costs.

Marketing:

The overall marketing budget is set by head office without consultation with restaurant managers. Veggie Delights has marketing managers who have responsibility for different channels – for example, Gill Evans looks at traditional advertising through local newspapers and leaflets sent to target areas by post, whereas Jenni Black is responsible for online marketing through the website and social media.

Each year the total marketing budget is set, taking account of new restaurants and new menus that Veggie Delights wishes to promote. No account is taken of the previous year's spend. However, it is up the marketing managers to then estimate what effect this marketing spend might have on their areas of interest.

The marketing department provide sales trend analysis based on regression analysis, which produces a straight-line relationship between the marketing spend and sales volumes for previous periods.

Provide a 'SWOT' analysis of the above budget process and recommend, where appropriate changes to this process. (15 marks)

Note:

A 'strength' is where you feel the process is good and a 'weakness' is where you feel the process is not so good. An 'opportunity' to improve the process may exist in places and a 'threat' is best written as a bad consequence of a poor budget process.

Strengths
Weaknesses
Opportunities
Threats

TASK 1.3

Assessment objective 3	Evaluate an organisation's accounting control systems and procedures.

Note: in the two sample assessments task 1.3 only asked for weaknesses and explanations of implications. In two of the tasks here, we have also asked for recommendations as this is also useful practice for task 6.

25 VEGGIE DELIGHTS' PURCHASING SYSTEM

Below is a description of the purchasing and payments system for Veggie Delights in respect of food and drinks costs in its restaurants.

Ordering

Whenever new food or drink supplies are required, the relevant restaurant manager sends a requisition form to the ordering department. An order clerk raises a purchase order and contacts a number of suppliers to see which can despatch the goods first. This supplier is then chosen. The order clerk sends out the purchase order. This is not sequentially numbered and only orders above £100 require authorisation.

Bookkeeping

Purchase invoices are input daily by the purchase ledger clerk, who has been in the role for many years and, as an experienced team member, he does not apply any application controls over the input process. Every week the purchase day book automatically updates the purchase ledger, the purchase ledger is then posted manually to the general ledger by the purchase ledger clerk.

Payments

Veggie Delights maintains a current account and a number of saving (deposit) accounts. The current account is reconciled weekly but the saving (deposit) accounts are only reconciled every two months.

In order to maximise their cash and bank balance, Veggie Delights has a policy of delaying payments to all suppliers for as long as possible. Suppliers are paid by a bank transfer. The finance director is given the total amount of the payments list, which she authorises and then processes the bank payments.

Required:

Identify and explain FOUR deficiencies in the system, explain the possible implication of each deficiency and provide a recommendation to address each deficiency. (15 marks)

Weakness	**Implication**	**Recommendation**

26 VEGGIE DELIGHTS' CASH RECEIPTS AND PAYMENTS PROCESSES

Below is a description of the cash receipts and payments system used by Veggie Delights.

The purchasing department based at the company's head office is responsible for ordering food and beverages for all six restaurants. In addition, each restaurants has a petty cash float of £400, held in the safe, which is used for the purchase of sundry items. When making purchases of sundries, employees are required to obtain the funds from the restaurant manager, purchase the sundries and return any excess money and the receipt to the manager. At any time the petty cash sum held and receipts should equal the float of £400 but it has been noted that on some occasions this has not been the case.

Each restaurant has five cash tills (cash registers) to take payments from customers. Three are located in the bar area and two in the restaurant area. Customers can pay using either cash or a credit card and for any transaction either the credit card vouchers or cash are placed in the till by the employee operating the till. To speed up the payment process, each venue has a specific log on code which can be used to access all five tills and is changed every two weeks.

At each venue at the end of the day, the tills are closed down by the restaurant manager who counts the total cash in all five tills and the sum of the credit card vouchers and these totals are reconciled with the aggregated daily readings of sales taken from each till. Any discrepancies are noted on the daily sales sheet. The daily sales sheet records the sales per the tills, the cash counted and the total credit card vouchers as well as any discrepancies. These sheets are scanned and emailed to the cashier, Tommy Mills, at head office at the end of each week.

Approximately 30% of Veggie Delights' customers pay in cash for their restaurant or bar bills. Cash is stored in the safe at each venue on a daily basis after the sales reconciliation has been undertaken. Each safe is accessed via a key which the restaurant manager has responsibility for. Each key is stored in a drawer of the manager's desk when not being used. Cash is transferred to the bank via daily collection by a security company.

The security company provides a receipt for the sums collected, and these receipts are immediately forwarded to head office. The credit card company remits the amounts due directly into Veggie Delights' bank account within two days of the transaction.

At head office, on receipt of the daily sales sheets and security company receipts, the cashier agrees the cash transferred by the security company has been banked for all venues. He agrees the cash per the daily sales sheets to bank deposit slips and to the bank statements. The cashier updates the cash book with the cash banked and details of the credit card vouchers from the daily sales sheets. On a monthly basis, the credit card company sends a statement of all credit card receipts from the six venues which is filed by the cashier.

Every two months, the cashier reconciles the bank statements to the cash book. The reconciliations are reviewed by the financial controller, Amar Hemeer who evidences his review by signature and these are filed in the accounts department. All purchases of food and beverages for the venues are paid by bank transfer. At the relevant payment dates, the finance director, Agnes Copeland, is given the total amount of the payments list which she authorises.

Required:

Identify and explain FIVE DEFICIENCIES in Veggie Delights' cash receipts and payments system and provide a recommendation to address each of these deficiencies. (15 marks)

Control deficiency	Recommendation

27 VEGGIE DELIGHTS' INVENTORY COUNTING PROCESSES

Each winter, Veggie Delights is obliged to count its inventory in its restaurants. This is typically done on the morning of the 1st January.

For a restaurant, inventory is held in a number of different places. Each restaurant typically has a large fridge-freezer and a cupboard for storing unused food and drinks. In addition, bottles of drinks, some part empty in the case of spirits, are held in the bar area and a variety of other ingredients, such as flour, olive oil and spices are kept in the kitchen.

Each restaurant manager organises the inventory count at their own restaurant using their permanent staff. In addition, this year, Veggie Delights arranged for an internal auditor to attend some of the inventory counts and feedback their findings. It was hoped that this would lead to improved procedures in the future. In one restaurant, the local staff were short numbered and so the internal auditor acted as a counter and an auditor at the same time.

Each restaurant count was split into two teams. The first would count goods in the fridge-freezer and the second the cupboard. Then, depending on how fast each team counted, the final zones (bar and kitchen area) could be dealt with.

For each restaurant, sales information is detailed enough for head office to prepare pre-printed inventory sheets showing expected inventory levels for drinks and packaged goods, such as crisps, so staff are expected to count these items and tick the relevant box if quantities match. Where there is a disagreement, the revised quantity should be added.

For some items, such as fruits, vegetables, eggs, herbs and spices, sales information does not allow head office to calculate exactly what quantities should be present. For these goods a sheet of all possible products is generated and staff expected to complete the quantities.

Suppliers were requested not to deliver during the inventory counts. This policy was mostly followed but one supplier of frozen vegetables failed to obey and a delivery was made to three restaurants. The drivers offloaded the stock in the car park and left so as not to interfere with the counting process.

During the count, boxes of drinks not yet unpacked were not opened but the slips on the side of the boxes were used to note the contents on the inventory sheets.

Goods were not individually checked for 'best by' or 'use by' dates but staff were asked to make a note of any items that looked 'past their best'.

Outline 5 weaknesses and their effect on the accounting systems in the boxes below:
(15 marks)

Weakness	Effect of Weakness

Weakness	**Effect of Weakness**

TASK 1.4

Assessment objective 4	Analyse an organisation's decision making and control using management accounting tools.

28 RESTAURANT MENU DECISIONS

Veggie Delights has expanded its vegan menu choices and these have been extremely popular. One particular range utilises a rare Tibetan turnip that a local organic farmer has managed to grow successfully. The turnip has a world-wide reputation for its health benefits, particularly in terms of improving respiratory function, and Veggie Delights' meal options using it have received rave reviews on social media and in local newspapers.

The problem facing the business is that it can only acquire limited quantities of the turnip and restaurants have usually sold out of meals using it by half way through an evening sitting. Directors are considering alternative sources of supply but, in the meantime, have called a meeting to discuss how best to use the limited supplies

The following table provided shows the sales and profitability of four menu options for a typical restaurant in a single week.

Sales and profitability data

Meal option using the Tibetan turnip	**A**	**B**	**C**	**D**
Potential sales demand (meals)	25	30	20	40
	£	£	£	£
Selling price	15.00	12.00	12.50	10.00
Variable costs (ingredients)	10.00	8.00	7.00	5.00
Contribution per meal	**5.00**	**4.00**	**5.50**	**5.00**
Total contribution	125	120	110	200
Apportioned fixed overheads	(50)	(60)	(40)	(80)
Operating profit	**70**	**60**	**70**	**120**
Tibetan turnip usage per meal (grams)	100	96	120	110
Contribution per gram	**0.050**	**0.042**	**0.046**	**0.045**

Notes:

1 Loyalty card discounts have been excluded from the above selling prices.

2 Fixed overheads relate to restaurant labour, rent and energy costs. These are apportioned on a budgeted unit basis to assist decision making.

Directors' discussion

At the Board meeting, the directors gave their views as to which of the four menu options should be made if turnip supplies were limited.

Sean O'Keefe, the Managing Director, argued that, based on total operating profits, meal D should be offered on the menu. His argument was that the apportioned fixed overhead had to be taken into account as it had to be covered somewhere in the business.

Caroline Rowley, the Deputy Managing Director, disagreed. Her opinion was that the allocated fixed costs were irrelevant and that they should just look at the contribution, although she was unclear whether it was better to look at contribution per meal (and pick C) or total contribution (and pick D).

Agnes Copeland, the Finance Director, thought the correct approach was to look at the contribution per gram of Tibetan turnip as they had limited ingredients, rather than the total or unit contribution. She thus favoured meal A.

(a) BRIEFLY discuss the validity of each of the three directors' views on how the final decision should be made as to which meal options to prioritise. (9 marks)

Managing Director
Deputy Managing Director
Finance Director

(b) BRIEFLY explain TWO other factors should be taken into consideration before making a final decision. (6 marks)

Factor 1

Factor 2

29 NEW SUPPLIERS

Veggie Delights is considering extending its product range to include merchandising. The goods will consist of a range of toys made from sustainable materials. The toys will be based on the vegetables that are contained within the children's menu.

As part of this, a suitable supplier needs to be chosen. The decision is to be based on a range of factors, both financial and non-financial.

The financial argument will be based simply on cost. Veggie Delights is keen to introduce target costing to achieve a minimum 60% mark up and it is felt that suppliers should be chosen that help Veggie Delights achieve this.

Non-financial factors will focus on quality – both that of the product offered and the quality of the service provided.

To help collect information for making the decision, one of the toys, a lovable tomato named Bob, will be used as an example. Veggie Delights wants the toys made with double stitching throughout for added strength and from recyclable materials.

(a) Which of the following prices should be used for target costing? (2 marks)

The budgeted price that Veggie Delights has set for 20Y0	
The existing price that Veggie Delights uses	
The market average price	
The price charged by Veggie Delights' main competitor for a similar toy	

(b) Calculate the target cost for a large Bob toy using the information below. **(3 marks)**

Cost per unit	£
Production cost (charged by supplier)	
Transportation costs (paid by Veggie Delights)	0.05
Total cost	
Mark up (60%)	
Target selling price	3.20

(c) Briefly explain how the concept of value analysis applies to Veggie Delights and the options available to it to close any cost gap. **(4 marks)**

Value analysis
Options available to Veggie Delights

(d) Information for three potential suppliers of the Bob toy is given as follows:

Supplier	A	B	C
Production cost	£2.00	£1.80	£1.60
Offers price discounts for bulk orders	Yes	No	No
Typical delivery time (weeks)	3	4	7
Typical credit terms (days)	30	60	45
Double stitching used throughout	Yes	No	No
Recyclable materials used throughout	Yes	Yes	No

Discuss which supplier should be chosen by referring to both financial and non-financial factors. **(6 marks)**

Financial factors
Non-financial factors

30 VEGGIE DELIGHTS' PLANNING

The sales of one of Veggie Delights' signature vegetarian meals has been in steady decline and questions are being raised about its long-term future and whether it should be dropped from the menu. Directors' views are mixed as the mal won many awards five years ago.

The meal is priced at £25.00 per person and Veggie Delights makes a contribution margin on sales of 60% on this product. This margin only accounts for variable costs. If fixed costs are averaged over all products than this product's share would be £2,500 a quarter. It is not thought that there is any directly attributable fixed cost.

The reason for the decline is thought to be because rivals, and even supermarkets, have copied the recipe and sell their own versions. As a result the meal is no longer seen as innovative and customers feel the price is too high.

To help assess the decision to discontinue the range, data has been gathered by the sales team on the volume of sales of the meal concerned over the past two years split by quarters (8 quarters in total) and your help is being requested to provide interpretation of that data.

The data analysis was performed using regression techniques where:

$Y = a + bX$

Y is the sales volume and X is the relevant quarter number

The data started with quarter 2 in 20X7 (X = 1) and provided six quarters of data (up to X = 6). The *'b'* value was found to be –20 and the *'a'* value was 345 units

(a) Using the data above complete the following table: (7 marks)

Quarter Number (X)	Number of meals (Y)	Revenue £	Variable Cost £	Contribution £
1 (Q2 20X7)	350			
2 (Q3 20X7)	290			
3 (Q4 20X7)	266			
4 (Q1 20X8)	258			
5 (Q2 20X8)	246			
6 (Q3 20X8)	238			
7 (Q4 20X8)				
8 (Q1 20X9)				
9 (Q2 20X9)				
10 (Q3 20X9)				

(b) Briefly discuss the meaning of the value 'b' above and your findings using the data and comment on whether Veggie Delights, from a financial viewpoint, would want to continue to offer this meal up to and including quarter 3 20X9 (6 marks)

(c) Briefly discuss any non-financial considerations regarding the withdrawal of a particular range from sale. (2 marks)

TASK 1.5

Assessment objective 5	Analyse an organisation's decision making and control using ratio analysis.

31 OVERTRADING

Despite the company having significant cash reserves, Sean O'Keefe has expressed concerns that Veggie Delights' high growth rate (67% growth in the number of restaurants in 20Y0) may result in an overtrading position, where financial and other resources are insufficient for the rate of expansion.

To help assess the extent of this risk a range of ratios have been calculated to create a scorecard based on Veggie Delights' forecast performance for 20Y0.

These are given below, together with some ratios from 20X9.

(a) Complete the scorecard by calculating the missing ratios. (10 marks)

VEGGIE DELIGHTS Scorecard	**20Y0**	**20X9**
Profitability and gearing		
Gross profit %	46.5%	48.8%
Operating profit %	6.6%	**%**
Return on capital employed	78.8%	**%**
Gearing (debt/equity)	0.35×	0.04×
Liquidity ratios		
Current ratio	1.78:1	1.08:1
Acid test/Quick ratio	1.46:1	**:1**
Working capital days		
Inventory holding period	4 days	**days**
Trade receivables collection period	3 days	0 days
Trade payables payment period	48 days	52 days
Working capital cycle	(41) days	**days**

(b) Select the ONE correct observation about each aspect of business performance below. **(10 marks)**

Profitability

20Y0 will be a year of steady, if unspectacular, progress. Although margins have dipped, the return on capital employed has been kept constant.	
The changes in gross margin could be due to cost control problems concerning distribution.	
Increased competition and the resulting pressure on prices could explain the change in each of the three profitability ratios.	

Gearing

The increased gearing ratio proves that the company has no problems raising additional debt finance.	
It is likely that the interest cover ratio has increased.	
The increased gearing ratio shows that the shareholders' position has become more risky.	

Liquidity

Both ratios have increased, which indicates that the company is less solvent.	
A higher quick ratio is a clear indicator of overtrading.	
The change in both the current and quick ratios could be partly explained by the increase in the receivables period.	

Working capital

The working capital cycle has worsened. This increases the possibility of Veggie Delights overtrading.	
There is a welcome improvement in the working capital cycle, mainly due to the change in the payment period for payables.	
The working capital cycle is worse than a year ago because of the change in inventory days.	

Overall performance

Despite overall growth, Veggie Delights is having a difficult year in 20Y0 and needs to investigate why key ratios are deteriorating.	
20Y0 looks to be a disaster for Veggie Delights.	
There is no evidence of possible control problems.	

32 COMPETITOR ANALYSIS

Joshua Edeki, the Finance Director, is preparing a presentation for the board of directors to discuss possible control problems within the business. He has asked you to complete a comparative 'score card' of key financial ratios comparing Veggie Delights and one of its rivals, which he will use as part of his presentation. The rival concerned has a chain of vegetarian restaurants and also owns and operates an organic farm.

Relevant data has been extracted for the rival as follows.

Extracts from accounts of Rival	**20X9** £000
Profitability	
Sales revenue	13,945
Cost of sales	7,070
Profit from operations	1,325
Assets	
Non-current assets	3,559
Inventories	1,162
Trade receivables	1,233
Total	**5,954**
Equities and liabilities	
Equity	3,958
Non-current liabilities – loans	792
Trade payables	581
Bank overdraft	423
Tax liabilities	200
Total	**5,954**

(a) Complete the scorecard by calculating the missing ratios. (10 marks)

20X9	**Veggie Delights**	**Rival**
Profitability		
Gross profit %	48.8%	
Operating profit %	7.8%	9.5%
Return on capital employed	116.6%	
Liquidity ratios		
Current ratio	1.1:1	
Acid test/Quick ratio	1.0:1	0.6:1

20X9	**Veggie Delights**	**Rival**
Working capital days		
Inventory holding period	6 days	60 days
Trade receivables collection period	0 days	32 days
Trade payables payment period	52 days	
Working capital cycle	(46) days	

(b) Assess the following statements and indicate whether they are true or false.

(10 marks)

Statement	*True*	*False*
The difference in gross margins could be explained by the Rival giving vouchers in promotions to increase customer numbers in its restaurants.		
If Veggie Delights has delayed paying suppliers at the year end, then this would contribute to the difference in current ratios.		
The difference in the lengths of the working capital cycles is more likely to be due to the rival's farming activities than its restaurants.		
A restaurant employee in Veggie Delights was found to have stolen bar snacks and given them to friends. This would contribute to the difference in the ROCE figures.		
Inadequate controls over expense claims for managers within Veggie Delights could contribute to the difference in the operating margins figures.		

33 CASH AND PROFIT

The directors of Veggie Delights have been having a discussion on the financial ratios of the business and which should take priority for the business.

Sean O'Keefe (Managing Director) stated "All that seems to matter is profit and profit-based ratios. Every time I watch a business program on television, profit is pretty much the first thing that is talked about." It is for this reason that I have instructed the accounts department to delay the payment of our next rent bills. This should increase our profitability at a vital time as I am meeting a team of venture capitalists soon to discuss future funding.

Caroline Rowley (Deputy Managing Director) in part agreed but added "I feel that cash flow and liquidity ratios are also vital. Surely the venture capitalists would be interested in how much cash we generate as well? However, at the end of the day cash and profit seem to be the same thing. I spend money on materials or wages and the same figure ends up in the profit and loss account, so if we are profitable we must have more cash coming in that going out."

Agnes Copeland (Finance Director) is a little despairing of her friends and colleagues and has asked you summarise the issue of 'profits versus cash' for her to use at the next board meeting where she will attempt to explain.

Briefly explain the profits and cash issues mentioned above under the following headings:

Why is profit important in business? (5 marks)
Why must cash also be considered in business? (5 marks)
Does the cash equal the profit? (5 marks)
Discuss whether delaying the rent payment will be effective in increasing profits and the ethical stance the accounting department should take to the request. (5 marks)

TASK 1.6

Assessment objective 6	Analyse the internal controls of an organisation and make recommendations.

34 VEGGIE DELIGHTS' PAYROLL SYSTEMS

You are currently reviewing the payroll systems of Veggie Delights.

As Veggie Delights is a small company it is not considered necessary to issue a contract of employment to every new member of staff in restaurants, especially waiting and bar staff, as some only want to work part time or for a limited period. Instead, each new starter in a restaurant is told verbally what their hours of work and rate of pay will be along with other key terms and conditions.

At the start of a shift, each employee uses a clock card to record their time of arrival. They use the same machine to clock out at the end of their shift. The clock machine is in a quiet corner of each restaurant, away from customers and kitchen, to avoid disruption. The clocking in and out process is not supervised. The rack where the clock cards are kept always contains one or two spare cards in case any get spoiled or damaged by the machine. Once an employee has clocked in, they are entitled to sit and have a drink and something to eat before starting work.

At the end of each week, the restaurant manager collects the clock cards from the rack in each cafe and posts them to the Payroll Manager at head office, Nelson Badar.

Customers often leave a gratuity for the staff when they pay their bill. These gratuities are left by the customer in a dish by the cash register and at the end of each month the cafe manager divides the amount by the total hours worked by each employee and gives them their share in cash. No records of these amounts are retained.

Customers pay for their food and drink at the central cash register in each cafe, either by cash or payment card. The cash register is pre-programmed with the price of each menu item including if they attract sales tax or not, and these prices can only be adjusted by the restaurant manager concerned. At the end of each day, the cash register produces a total of sales, split between cash and card amounts. Sales are recorded in the accounting system analysed by restaurant and by payment method. On a daily basis the restaurant manager counts the physical cash in the register and produces a report from the card machine and reconciles the total cash and credit card payments to the total sales figure from cash register report.

Although there are usually four members of staff serving customers during any shift, only the restaurant manager and one other person per shift are authorised to use the cash register and take payments from customers.

There is a CCTV camera positioned above the cash register recording during the opening times of each cafe.

Identify and explain FIVE DEFICIENCIES in Veggie Delights' payroll system, and provide a recommendation to address each of these deficiencies. (15 marks)

Deficiency	Recommendation

35 DALE FARM SALES AND DESPATCH SYSTEM

The Board of Veggie Delights are considering buying an organic farm. One potential target they have found is Dale Farm, which sells fruit and vegetables to supermarkets, restaurants, smaller retailers and cafes, and to the end consumer. The farm has a dedicated sales team to manage the relationship with larger restaurants and supermarkets but orders from smaller cafes, independent retailers and the public are mainly placed through Dale Farm's website, while some are also made via telephone.

Conor Seddon (Commercial Manager) has started to investigate the farm in more detail and has some concerns over its sales and despatch system. He is reasonably happy over the way restaurants and supermarkets are dealt with but has concerns over telephone and website transactions.

Online orders are automatically checked against inventory records and fruit and vegetable picking schedules for availability; telephone orders, however, are checked manually by order clerks after the call. A follow-up call is usually made to customers if there is insufficient inventory. When taking telephone orders, clerks note down the details on plain paper and afterwards they complete a three part pre-printed order form. These order forms are not sequentially numbered and are sent manually to both despatch and the accounts department.

As the company is expanding, customers are able to place online orders which will exceed their agreed credit limit by 10%. Online orders are automatically forwarded to the despatch and accounts department.

A daily pick list is printed by the despatch department and this is used by the warehouse team to despatch goods. The goods are accompanied by a despatch note and all customers are required to sign a copy of this. On return, the signed despatch notes are given to the warehouse team to file.

The sales quantities are entered from the despatch notes and the authorised sales prices are generated by the invoicing system. If a discount has been given, say for a bulk order, then this has to be manually entered by the sales clerk onto the invoice.

Due to the expansion of the company, and as there is a large number of sale invoices, extra accounts staff have been asked to help out temporarily with producing the sales invoices. Normally it is only two sales clerks who produce the sales invoices.

Identify and explain FIVE deficiencies in Dale Farm's sales and despatch system and provide a recommendation to address each of these deficiencies. (15 marks)

Deficiency	Recommendation

Deficiency	**Recommendation**

36 VEGGIE DELIGHTS' GENERAL LEDGER SYSTEM

Veggie Delights' general ledger is controlled by Agnes Copleand (Finance Director) and Amar Hameer (Financial Controller) with either of these people able to make independent journal entries. Agnes and Amar are friends and keen skiers and do like to get away over the winter period to ski in various parts of the world. This isn't always easy to arrange as the year-end work needs to finish quickly to enable this holiday to take place. Lauren Bristow (HR Director) is given access to the general ledger over this period in the unlikely event further adjustments are needed.

Agnes does not require prior sight of the journals prepared by Amar as there is considerable trust between the two.

Anyone with general ledger access can create new general ledger accounts.

Non-current assets accounting policy

During the current year, the approach taken to accounting for non-current assets has been investigated by Agnes. Having compared the approach taken by Veggie Delights to other similar restaurants, she has decided to change a couple of matters:

- Firstly, smaller restaurant and kitchen utensils would no longer be capitalised but, instead, written off as expenses.
- Secondly, the depreciation approach for larger kitchen items , such as ovens,

This decision was taken by Agnes just before her annual skiing holiday and so she instructed Lauren to make the appropriate adjustments.

Identify and explain five weaknesses in the general ledger system and suggest an improvement for each weakness to reduce the risk of error or misstatement. (15 marks)

Weakness	Suggestion for improvement

Weakness	**Suggestion for improvement**

Section 3

ANSWERS TO PRACTICE QUESTIONS

TASK 1.1

Assessment objective 1	Demonstrate an understanding of the roles and responsibilities of the accounting function within an organisation and examine ways of preventing and detecting fraud and systemic weaknesses.

1 STATUTORY DUTY

Who has the statutory duty to prepare accounts for Veggie Delights?

The company auditors.	
The directors of the company.	✓
Finance Director.	
Financial Controller.	
Companies House.	

2 RESPONSIBILITY

Who is responsible for maintaining sound risk management and internal control systems within Veggie Delights?

The company auditors.	
The directors of the company.	✓
Finance Director.	
Financial Controller.	
Companies House.	

3 BANK RECONCILIATION 1

Adjustment	*Amount* £	*Debit/Credit*
Adjustment for (2)	106	Cr
Adjustment for (3)	350	Dr
Adjustment for (4)	1,645	Dr

Note:

Reconciliation

Cash book

Balance b/d	103	ADJUSTMENT (2)	106
ADJUSTMENT (3)	350		
ADJUSTMENT (4)	1,645		
		Balance c/d	1,992
	2,098		2,098

Balance of bank account	363
Uncleared lodgements	1,629
	1,992

4 BANK RECONCILIATION 2

	Yes	No
A trade customer was accidentally invoiced twice for the same item.		✓
A trade customer took a 2% prompt payment discount despite not having paid within the timescales required to earn a discount.		✓
Bank interest received had not been posted to the cash book.	✓	
A payment to a supplier of £2,500 had accidentally been posted as £250.	✓	

5 SALES LEDGER CONTROL ACCOUNT RECONCILIATION 1

	Add/Subtract	£
Total from list of balances		1,100
Adjustment for (a)	Add	65
Adjustment for (b)	Subtract	280
Adjustment for (c)	Subtract	1,170
Adjustment for (d)	Add	3,600
Adjustment for (e)	Subtract	99
Adjustment for (f)	Subtract	100
Revised total to agree with SLCA		3,116

6 SALES LEDGER CONTROL ACCOUNT RECONCILIATION 2

	Yes	No
A trade customer was accidentally invoiced twice for the same item.		✓
A trade customer was sold items at the wrong price.		✓
Credit balances had been omitted from the list of receivables balances.	✓	
A payment from a customer of £230 had accidentally been posted as £320 to their individual account in the receivables ledger.	✓	

7 PURCHASES LEDGER CONTROL ACCOUNT RECONCILIATION

	Add/Subtract	£
Total from list of balances		132,589
Adjustment for (a)	Add	445
Adjustment for (b)	Subtract	4,340
Adjustment for (c)	Subtract	1,200
Adjustment for (d)	Subtract	132
Adjustment for (e)	Add	2,100
Adjustment for (f)	Add	120
Revised total to agree with PLCA		129,582

8 ERRORS

(a) Journal

	Dr £	*Cr* £
Motor expenses	4,500	
Motor vehicles at cost		4,500

(b) Journal

	Dr £	*Cr* £
Office sundries	16	
Suspense		16

(c) Journal

	Dr £	*Cr* £
Closing inventory – statement of financial position	42,000	
Closing inventory – statement of profit or loss		42,000

Working

Inventory is valued at the lower of cost and net realisable value. The selling price is given as £50,400. To get to the selling price, 20% of the value of the cost is added to the cost. The cost of £42,000 has been calculated by dividing the selling price by 120 and then multiplying by 100. (50,400/120) × 100 = 42,000.

The value of closing inventory, in accordance with IAS 2 is £42,000.

(d) Journal

	Dr £	*Cr* £
Receivables	1,720	
Discounts allowed		1,720
Discounts allowed	1,270	
Receivables		1,270

9 CHANGEOVER

Which TWO of the following controls can mitigate the risk of system failure during direct changeover?

Testing	✓
Training	
System documentation	
Data backup	✓
Check digits	

Note: Testing reduces the probability of failure, and data backup reduces the impact.

10 INFORMATION SYSTEM CONTROLS

	Security	Integrity
Locked doors	✓	
Passwords	✓	
Batch totals		✓
Reconciliation		✓
CCTV	✓	
Check digits		✓
Authorisation of data entry		✓
Fire alarms	✓	

11 PURCHASE CYCLE CONTROLS 1

Which TWO of the following controls in a purchase cycle could be implemented to reduce the risk of payment of goods not received?

Sequentially pre-numbered purchase requisitions and sequence check.	
Matching of goods received note with purchase invoice.	✓
Goods are inspected for condition and quantity and agreed to purchase order before acceptance.	✓
Daily update of inventory system.	

12 PURCHASE CYCLE CONTROLS 2

Which TWO of the following controls in the purchase cycle could be implemented to reduce the risk of procurement of unnecessary goods and services?

Centralised purchasing department.	✓
Sequentially pre-numbered purchase requisitions and sequence check.	
Orders can only be placed with suppliers from the approved suppliers list.	
All purchase requisitions are signed as authorised by an appropriate manager.	✓

13 EXPENSE CLAIM CONTROLS

Which ONE of the following essential internal control measures is evidently missing from Veggie Delights Ltd?

Veggie Delights lacks a control environment as the board are not setting an ethical tone at the top.	✓
Veggie Delights lacks an Internal Audit department.	
Veggie Delights lacks an experienced finance manager.	
Veggie Delights lacks an external auditor.	

14 PASSWORDS 1

Which of the following would be the most secure?

24june1963	
LaraJo	
mypassword	
Qwerty123!#	✓

15 PASSWORDS 2

Which TWO of the following would reduce the effectiveness of passwords?

Requirement that passwords are changed every two weeks	
Users are allowed to choose their own passwords	✓
Automatic lock-out after 3 failed attempts to access system	
Making the sharing of passwords a disciplinary offence	
Displaying the password on the screen when entered	✓

16 INTERNAL CONTROLS 1

Match each of the following activities to the component that it illustrates.

	Control environment	Information system	Control activities
The process of preparing the financial statements		✓	
Locking the inventory storeroom			✓

17 INTERNAL CONTROLS 2

Match each of the following activities to the type of control that it illustrates.

	Authorisation	Information processing	Physical control
The financial controller will count petty cash on a weekly basis			✓
There will be two keys to the locked safe: one held by the FD and the other by the MD.			✓

18 INTERNAL CONTROLS 3

Match each of the following activities to the type of computer control that it illustrates.

	General	Application
Storing extra copies of programs and data files off-site	✓	
New programmes to check data fields on input transactions		✓
Manual checks to ensure that input data were authorised		✓
Password protection limiting access to data	✓	
Range checks on payroll processing		✓
Manual checks to ensure that timesheets are authorised before details are processed		✓

19 INTERNAL CONTROLS 4

Indicate whether the following limitations are true or false.

	True	False
The cost of implementing controls may be more expensive than the benefits gained due to reduced risk	✓	
The effectiveness of many controls rely on the integrity of those applying them	✓	
Internal controls are only applied to material items		✓
Standard controls may not be designed to deal with unusual transactions	✓	

20 FRAUD 1

Which TWO of the following would best reduce the risk of this fraud occurring?

Segregation of duties between cash payments and recording at head office	
Post opening by two people	
Daily reconciliation of recorded till sales and cash taken within restaurants	✓
Regular banking of cash and cheques received in restaurants	✓

21 FRAUD 2

Which ONE of the following control activities would best prevent this occurring?

Payroll standing data periodically printed out and checked on a line-by-line basis to independently held employee details	
Use of hierarchical passwords over standing data files	✓
Pre-authorisation of all amendments to payroll standing data by an independent official	
Supervision of the wages pay out by an independent official	

Note: In order to prevent this from happening, the key is that fictitious employees never make it onto the payroll.

- Printing out and checking standing data will detect any fictitious employees added but will not prevent them from being added.
- Use of hierarchical passwords over standing data files ensures that an unscrupulous employee cannot access the part of the system where new employees would be added and hence will prevent the fraud. This is therefore the correct answer.
- Pre-authorisation of all amendments will not prevent the addition as an unscrupulous employee will not ask for authorisation but will simply add the fictitious details if the system allows them to do this.
- Supervision of the wages pay out by an independent official might detect dummy employees but would be unlikely to prevent the fraud.

TASK 1.2

Assessment objective 2	Evaluate budgetary reporting; its effectiveness in controlling and improving organisational performance.

22 TRAINING COSTS

(a) **BRIEFLY discuss THREE weaknesses in the above use of performance reports to improve the focus of training within Veggie Delights.**

Weakness 1

Flexing

The budget is a fixed one; meaning it has not been flexed for the 25% increase in activity.

A flexible budget is one where the turnover and variable costs are changed in line with the change in activity. In this case they would be increased by 25%. Fixed costs remain unchanged from the original budget.

The advantage of fixed budgeting is that it takes less time and is, therefore, less costly to produce; the disadvantage is that variances are less meaningful and, therefore, control is effectively reduced. The advantage and disadvantage of flexible budgeting are the opposite of this.

The flexed budget cost would be

$$13,000 + 1,000 \times (25/20) = £14,250$$

This gives an overall favourable variance of £150 rather than an adverse one of £100. The manager should thus be praised rather than reprimanded.

Weakness 2
Participation in target setting and budgeting Petr Higgs was not involved in setting the original budget and did not even know about it. This lack of participation could easily result in him viewing the target as unfair and unrealistic, resulting in demotivation. It is also very difficult to be motivated to hit a target you are unaware of! Greater participation will help resolve these issues and also may result in more realistic budgets in the first place. The main disadvantage of participation is the possibility of budget "padding", where Petr may have tried to set an easy target for himself.
Weakness 3
Emphasis on financial factors The sole emphasis on financial factors only may result in Petr being more concerned about cost control than delivering high quality training. The directors were concerned that training lacked focus rather than it being too expensive. There is nothing in the email to see if focus has improved.
Weakness 4
Mark Austin's tone Lauren Bristow's tone is far too aggressive, particularly given the above factors, and is likely to result in resentment and demotivation. This is particularly the case as it is the first month of the new system, so there is a significant possibility that budgeted figures are not representative in the first place. The variance could thus be due to planning errors rather than Petr's operational performance.

(b) Outline THREE performance indicators that could be used to assess the quality of the training provided.

Performance Indicator 1
Trainee feedback Trainees could be asked to score different elements of the training process on a score of 1 to 5 say. This would indicate whether or not they felt the training was useful to them and would indicate areas for improvement.
Performance Indicator 2
Manager feedback Presumably restaurant managers had objectives when sending staff on training courses/events – for example, to improve food hygiene processes. Managers could be asked to assess whether they felt that their staff had benefited from the training – for example, were they more able to undertake required tasks in their roles? Again, a score of 1 to 5 would allow easier monitoring of feedback.
Performance Indicator 3
Objective scoring using tests For some training – for example, awareness of food handling and hygiene legislation – it may be possible to set a quiz or test before and after training to see if trainee's knowledge and awareness had improved.

(Total 15 marks)

23 BUDGETING

Evaluate the budget for 20Y0 by discussing the following assumed (or implied) growth rates and margins. In your answer discuss whether or not you feel the figures are realistic and why. **(15 marks)**

Figure	Whether or not realistic
Sales volume growth of 25.0%	*Arguments for* Growth in customer numbers of 25% seems reasonable, given the plan to increase the number of restaurants by 66.7% and increasing brand awareness due to the award. The fact that growth is lower than the increase in the number of restaurants may be due to openings being staggered and the fact that new restaurants will take some time to build up customers. *Arguments against* However, the budgeted growth is higher than the industry forecast of 10-15%, suggesting the target is only achievable if market share is gained from rivals. Furthermore, the number of rivals offering vegan options is likely to increase, making it harder to defend, let alone gain market share
Sales revenue growth of 20.0%	Compared to volume growth of 25%, sales growth of 20% seems even more reasonable. The difference is due to the average spend per customer decreasing by 3.9%. This could be due to a fall in the average price, due to a cut in prices to attract new customers or price cuts as a response to increased competition, or due to a change is sales mix – for example, more customers eating at lunchtime rather than in the evening.
Cost of sales growth of 17.0%	Cost of sales growth of only 17% seems low compared to sales volume growth of 25%. One way of explaining this difference between them would only be feasible if a significant proportion of cost of sales were fixed costs rather than variable. This seems likely as the main part of cost of sales will be the labour cost of restaurant staff Another explanation could be that, having more restaurants, the company is able to benefit from additional economies of scale, such as discounts, when sourcing food.
Fall in operating expenses of 1.3%	Operating costs are likely to be mainly fixed in nature, so the only way a decrease can be achieved would be as a result of cost efficiencies. There is no information to suggest that such cost savings are feasible. If anything, one would expect having 4 more restaurants to increase admin costs at head office, rather than seeing savings.

Conclusion – whether or not the budget is realistic

Overall the budget looks reasonable in terms of sales growth and cost behaviour, especially if plans to open new restaurants are fully implemented in time to impact the budget to the degree shown.

24 VEGGIE DELIGHTS' BUDGETING PROCESS

Strengths

- Inflation should be allowed for as this leads to more accurate budgets
- Food costs seem to be accounted for correctly
- Marketing seems to be based on only those areas that the directors wish to specifically promote, reducing the possibility of cost overspends or unfocussed marketing expenditure
- Some attempt is made to account for the effectiveness of the marketing spend using regression analysis

Weaknesses

- Whilst choice over RPI and CPI is good for motivation it can lead to inconsistency and confusion for managers that are unaware of the difference and appropriateness of these.
- No inflationary guidance is given for costs other than wages, rents and food implying that these other costs are "minor". This therefore excludes, for example, energy costs, which are significant.
- Past inflation is not necessarily equal to future inflation – for example, after the Brexit vote in the UK, inflation jumped considerably compared to past measures
- Rent might not be affected by inflation at all. Leases have fixed rent review points and can sometimes be influenced by general market condition as well as inflation
- Restaurant managers are not consulted on any local marketing need. This can be demotivating and might not address concerns over poor performance – for example, a new rival may have opened near an existing restaurant but senior management may be unaware of the threat
- It is unclear how total budgets are allocated – for example, Jenni Black may feel that Veggie Delights needs to spend more promoting its online presence
- Past marketing to sales trends may not continue given the ever-changing markets
- Sales volumes change for other reasons (not just marketing)

Opportunities

- A central decision should be made regarding the inflation measure to be used
- More complete inflationary guidance could be given to include all costs lines
- Guidance could be given concerning rental budgets, suggesting that existing leases be reviewed for rent revision dates
- Greater account could be given to current market conditions when predicting sales (rather than relying purely on past regression)

Threats
• If inflation is under estimated on a cost then this could lead to an under budgeted costs and adverse variances. The opposite is true for overestimated inflation • Omission of inflationary guidance for (in particular) cost of sales could lead to a significant budget error, loss of confidence in the process and under funding • Sales levels may disappoint if no local considerations are made • Assuming that the past will continue into the future is misguided and new opportunities may be missed or complacency could set in • Budget sales levels could be incorrect leading to poor assumptions about profitability

TASK 1.3

Assessment objective 3	Evaluate an organisation's accounting control systems and procedures.

25 VEGGIE DELIGHTS' PURCHASING SYSTEM

Required:

Identify and explain FOUR deficiencies in the system, explain the possible implication of each deficiency and provide a recommendation to address each deficiency. (15 marks)

Deficiency	**Implication**	**Recommendation**
When raising purchase orders, the clerks choose whichever supplier can dispatch the goods the fastest.	This could result in Veggie Delights ordering goods at a much higher price or a lower quality than they would like, as the only factor considered was speed of delivery. It is important that goods are dispatched promptly, but this is just one of many criteria that should be used in deciding which supplier to use.	An approved supplier list should be compiled; this should take into account the price of goods, their quality and also the speed of delivery. Once the list has been produced, all orders should only be placed with suppliers on the approved list.

Purchase orders are not sequentially numbered.	Failing to sequentially number the orders means that Veggie Delights' ordering team is unable to monitor if all orders are being fulfilled in a timely manner; this could result in stock outs. If the orders are numbered, then a sequence check can be performed for any unfulfilled orders.	All purchase orders should be sequentially numbered and on a regular basis a sequence check of unfulfilled orders should be performed.
Purchase orders below £100 are not authorised and are processed solely by an order clerk.	This can result in goods being purchased which are not required by Veggie Delights. In addition, there is an increased fraud risk as an order clerk could place orders for personal goods up to the value of £100, which is significant.	All purchase orders should be authorised by a responsible official. Authorised signatories should be established with varying levels of purchase order authorisation.
Purchase invoices are input daily by the purchase ledger clerk and due to his experience, he does not utilise any application controls.	Without application controls there is a risk that invoices could be input into the system with inaccuracies or they may be missed out entirely. This could result in suppliers being paid incorrectly or not all, leading to a loss of supplier goodwill.	The purchase ledger clerk should input the invoices in batches and apply application controls, such as control totals, to ensure completeness and accuracy over the input of purchase invoices.
The purchase day book automatically updates with the purchase ledger but this ledger is manually posted to the general ledger.	Manually posting the amounts to the general ledger increases the risk of errors occurring. This could result in the payables balance in the financial statements being under or overstated.	The process should be updated so that on a regular basis the purchase ledger automatically updates the general ledger. A responsible official should then confirm through purchase ledger control account reconciliations that the update has occurred correctly.

Veggie Delights' saving (deposit) bank accounts are only reconciled every two months.	If these accounts are only reconciled periodically, there is the risk that errors will not be spotted promptly. Also, this increases the risk of employees committing fraud. If they are aware that these accounts are not regularly reviewed, then they could use these cash sums fraudulently.	All bank accounts should be reconciled on a regular basis, and at least monthly, to identify any unusual or missing items. The reconciliations should be reviewed by a responsible official and they should evidence their review.
Veggie Delights has a policy of delaying payments to their suppliers for as long as possible.	Whilst this maximises Veggie Delights' bank balance, there is the risk that Veggie Delights is missing out on early settlement discounts. Also, this can lead to a loss of supplier goodwill as well as the risk that suppliers may refuse to supply goods to Veggie Delights or send lower quality food.	Veggie Delights should undertake cash flow forecasting/ budgeting to maximise bank balances. The policy of delaying payment should be reviewed, and suppliers should be paid in a systematic way, such that supplier goodwill is not lost.

26 VEGGIE DELIGHTS' CASH RECEIPTS AND PAYMENTS PROCESSES

Required:

Identify and explain FIVE DEFICIENCIES in Veggie Delights' cash receipts and payments system and provide a recommendation to address each of these deficiencies. (15 marks)

Control deficiency	Recommendation
Each restaurant maintains a petty cash float of £400, and at any point in time the receipts and funds present should equal the float. It has been noted that on occasions there are differences due to the fact that no log is maintained of petty cash requests. This could be as a result of sundry items being purchased without the relevant receipt or voucher being returned. There is also a possibility that the cash is being misappropriated by staff members, or being spent on non-business related items.	A petty cash log should be maintained so the purchase of sundry items is recorded in the log along with the sum borrowed, date and employee. On purchase of the items, the relevant employee should return the relevant receipt or voucher and any funds not spent. The log should be updated to confirm return of funds and receipts. On a weekly basis, the restaurant manager should reconcile the petty cash and if any receipts are missing, these should be followed up with the relevant employee. If it is cash which is missing, then this should be investigated further with the employees who made petty cash purchases during that period.

Control deficiency	**Recommendation**
To speed up the cash payment by customers, for each venue the tills have the same log on code and these codes are changed fortnightly. In the event of cash discrepancies arising in the tills, it would be difficult to ascertain which employees may be responsible as there is no way of tracking who used which till. This could lead to cash being easily misappropriated.	Each employee should be provided with a unique log on code and this is required to be entered when using the tills. In order to facilitate the investigation of till differences, employees should be allocated to a specific till point for their shift. Any discrepancies which arise should initially be double checked to ensure they are not arithmetical errors. If still present, the relevant employees who had access to the till can be identified and further investigations can be undertaken.
The reconciliations of the tills to the daily sales readings are performed in total for all five tills at each venue rather than for each till. This means that when exceptions arise, it will be difficult to identify which till caused the difference. This increases the risk of staff undertaking fraudulent transactions.	The reconciliations should be undertaken on an individual till by till basis rather than in aggregate and any discrepancies noted should be investigated immediately. Furthermore, employees may require further till training.
The cashing up of tills along with the recording of any cash discrepancies is undertaken by just one individual, the restaurant manager. There is a fraud risk as the manager could remove some of the cash and then simply record that there was an exception on the daily sales list. In addition, as there is no segregation of duties, the restaurant manager could, fraudulently or by error, record the total sales as per each till incorrectly leading to incorrect identification of discrepancies.	The cashing up process should be undertaken by two individuals together, ideally an assistant manager and the restaurant manager. One should count the cash and the other record it. Any exceptions to the till reading should be double checked to confirm that they are not simply arithmetical errors. If still present, the relevant employees who had access to the till can be identified and further investigations can be undertaken.
Daily sales sheets are scanned and emailed to head office on a weekly basis. There is a possibility that some sales sheets could be misplaced by the restaurant manager. This will result in incomplete sales and cash receipts data being recorded into the accounting system.	Daily sales sheets for each venue should be sequentially numbered and remitted to head office on a daily basis. At head office, a sequence check should be undertaken on a regular basis to identify any missing sheets and any gaps should be investigated further. Once received, the cashier should post the sales and cash data for all six venues on a daily basis. Once processed, they should then be signed as posted by the cashier and filed away securely.

Control deficiency	**Recommendation**
Cash is stored in a safe at each venue and the restaurant manager stores the safe key in a drawer of their desk when not in use. Although cash is banked on a daily basis, there could still be a significant sum of cash onsite each day. There is a risk of significant cash losses due to theft if access to the safe key is not carefully controlled.	The current key lock safe should be replaced with a safe with a digital code. Only authorised personnel should have the code which should be updated on a regular basis.
The cashier is responsible for several elements of the cash receipts system. He receives the daily sales sheets from restaurants, agrees that cash has cleared into the bank statements, updates the cash book and undertakes the bank reconciliations. There is a lack of segregation of duties and errors will not be identified on a timely basis.	These key roles should be split between different members of the finance team, with ideally the bank reconciliations being undertaken by another member of the team.
The cashier is not checking that payments made by credit card have resulted in cash being received by Veggie Delights. The credit card statements are not reviewed or reconciled, they are just filed away. There is a risk that receipts of cash by credit card may have been omitted and this would not be identified on a timely basis as the bank is only reconciled every two months. This may result in difficulties in resolving any discrepancies with the credit card company.	The cashier should reconcile the credit card vouchers per restaurant to the monthly statement received from the card company. The daily amounts per the statement should be agreed to the bank statement to ensure that all funds have been received. This reconciliation should be reviewed by a responsible official, such as the financial controller, who should evidence by signature that the review has been undertaken.
The bank reconciliations are only carried out every two months. For a cash-based business, the bank reconciliation is a key control which reduces the risk of fraud and identifies errors. If it is not reconciled regularly enough, then this reduces its effectiveness as fraud and errors may not be identified on a timely basis.	The bank reconciliations should be performed on a monthly basis rather than every two months. The financial controller should continue to review each reconciliation and evidence his review by way of signature on the bank reconciliation.

Control deficiency	Recommendation
The finance director only views the total amount of payments to be made rather than the amounts to be paid to each supplier. Without looking at the detail of the payments list, as well as supporting documentation, there is a risk that suppliers could be being paid an incorrect amount, or that sums are being paid to fictitious suppliers. This will cause loss for the company.	The finance director should review the whole payments list prior to authorising. As part of this, she should agree the amounts to be paid to supporting documentation, as well as reviewing the supplier names to identify any duplicates or any unfamiliar names. She should evidence her review by signing the bank transfer list.

Note: only FIVE required.

27 VEGGIE DELIGHTS' INVENTORY COUNTING PROCESSES

Weakness	Effect of Weakness
The restaurant manager and staff should not be involved in the count at their own restaurant.	It would be very easy for a member of staff to cover up a fraud – for example, had they stolen a bottle of alcohol, then it would be easy to tick the inventory count sheet indicating the bottle was still in the store room. This would lead to an over-valuation of inventory.
The internal auditor should attend as an observer only and not get involved in the count itself. To do so confuses the roles of the people involved.	Errors in process might not have been detected as the internal auditor was busy "doing" rather than "observing". It is also possible that the internal auditor who is not an employee is not competent to recognize damaged or slow moving inventory and so these items could go unrecorded.
The designation of duties is a little unclear. The two unallocated zones appear to fall between two counting teams and so the count is then dependent on the organisation of the spare resource on the count day.	An area could either be missed or be counted by both teams. This could lead to over or under statement of the inventory and hence profit.
The instructions are capable of misinterpretation. When viewing a part used bottle of gin, say, it would be very difficult for staff to estimate how much was left in the bottle in order to match to records	Staff are likely to tick the drinks sheet as long as the observed levels are close to the records rather than performing more precise measurement. This could lead to overstatement of the inventory values.

Weakness	**Effect of Weakness**
There is no indication that staff sign or initial inventory sheets but are only asked to tick boxes.	Staff are less likely to take the check seriously (especially on 1st January) and there is no way of checking who ticked something if a discrepancy subsequently arises.
The delivery that took place on the day of the count might not have been accounted for properly. It is not clear from the question what happened to the actual counting of the delivery and whether staff included them in the count The details of items should have been noted down, even though they were in the car park at the time. Equally, details of the delivery should have been recorded so that correct cut off with regards to purchases could subsequently be checked.	The items could have been incorrectly included and so inventory overstated. Without delivery details being recorded a cut off error could have occurred. Consistency between the recording of inventory and the recording of purchases is important and without this the incorrect profit will be calculated. Also, if frozen goods were left in the car park then they could have thawed and become unfit for use.
Box labelling was relied on for the contents of unopened boxes. This is an unreliable method. Damaged items or wrong within the boxes would not be identified.	Inventory could be misstated as the content of the boxes might not reflect the labelling. If damaged items are not identified then the inventory will be overstated.
Old items were not adequately identified or recorded during the count. For example, an item in a fridge may look fine but be past its use by date and so unfit for use.	Inventory should be valued at the lower of cost and NRV. Food that is beyond its use by date should be disposed of and written down to zero. Inventory will thus be overvalued as a result.

Note: only FIVE required.

TASK 1.4

Assessment objective 4	Analyse an organisation's decision making and control using management accounting tools.

28 RESTAURANT MENU DECISIONS

(a) BRIEFLY discuss the validity of each of the three directors' views on how the final decision should be made as to meal options to prioritise. (9 marks)

Managing Director
The Managing Director is basing decisions on the reported profits of each product. The reported operating profits include an arbitrary allocation of fixed costs that undermines their credibility. While the Managing Director is correct that fixed costs must be covered somewhere, they are irrelevant to the decision as they are by definition unavoidable regardless of the decision. Decisions should be made on the basis of future incremental cash flows.
Deputy Managing Director
The Deputy Managing Director is basing decisions on the contribution of each product. This has the advantage of considering only the future relevant cash flows and ignoring the allocated fixed overheads. Looking at total contribution would only be appropriate if there was enough ingredients to make sufficient meals to meet full demand, which is not the case here. Unit contribution would be appropriate if all meals involved the same amount of Tibetan turnip, but, again, this is not the case here.
Finance Director
The Finance Director has the best overall approach as she is considering contribution, thus looking at relevant cash flows and ignoring allocated overheads. In addition, and unlike the Deputy Managing Director, she is then incorporating how much turnip is needed to make each meal. The ranking based on contribution per unit of scarce resource (i.e. grams of ingredient) should ensure that the use of Tibetan turnip is maximised to generate the most contribution possible.

(b) BRIEFLY explain THREE other factors should be taken into consideration before making a final decision. (6 marks)

Factor 1
How much turnip is available The decision is focussed on selecting just one meal to stock. However, it may be that there is sufficient turnip to offer a number of options, even if there is not enough for all of them. For example, making 400 Ds would need 40 × 110 = 4,400 grams. This is sufficient for all of the Cs (requires 20 × 102 = 2,400) and a significant number of Bs, say. Furthermore, it may be possible to increase the amount of available turnip by offering the farmer higher prices to be prioritised, although the premium paid would have to be factored into the contribution calculations.

Factor 2
Customer preferences Customers are likely to prefer having the full range of meal options offered rather than just one or two, and may be willing to come to the restaurants more often in order to taste all of them. Rather than simply offering two options, say, the company could consider rotating the choices to keep interest high.

29 NEW SUPPLIERS

(a) Which of the following prices should be used for target costing? (2 marks)

The budgeted price that Veggie Delights has set for 20Y0	✓
The existing price that Veggie Delights uses	
The market average price	
The price charged by Veggie Delights' main competitor for a similar toy	

(b) Calculate the target cost for a large satchel. (3 marks)

Cost per unit	£
Production cost (charged by supplier) = balancing figure	**1.95**
Transportation costs (given)	0.05
Total cost = 3.20 × 100/160	**2.00**
Mark up = 3.20 × 60/160	**1.20**
Target selling price	3.20

(c) Briefly explain how the concept of value analysis applies to Veggie Delights and the options available to it to close any cost gap. (4 marks)

Value analysis
Value analysis involves considering which aspects of the product are valued by the customer. This would allow Veggie Delights to identify possible areas for cutting costs to close any target cost 'gap' without compromising the value to the customer. For Veggie Delights the ultimate consumer will value the designs, ethical manufacturing and the brand, so these should not be compromised. However, customers may be less concerned about the quality of packaging or the stitching, so cost savings may be possible here.

Options available to Veggie Delights
Veggie Delights may be able to reduce transportation costs by choosing suppliers who are closer to key markets, rather than using foreign firms. Apart from this the only option is to get lower prices from suppliers, whether through cheaper materials or switching suppliers. Obviously it must be careful not to compromise customer perceived quality when doing this.

(d) Discuss which supplier should be chosen by referring to both financial and non-financial factors. (6 marks)

Financial factors
Target cost Both suppliers B and C meet the target cost criteria, with C being the cheapest. However, A may meet the target cost depending on the extent of any bulk discount offered. This may be not be significant as the toys may not achieve high sales.
Non-financial factors
Quality of supply The main problem with C is the long delivery time as this will either mean potential delays to customers or that mean that Veggie Delights will need to hold higher inventory levels. Delays to customers should be avoided given the importance of customer loyalty and satisfaction. On the other hand, holding more inventory will increase the length of the cash operating cycle. This may not be acceptable given high growth and associated fears regarding possible overtrading. Delivery times would favour A and B. Linked to cash flow problems we can also look at credit terms. Longer credit terms take the pressure off Veggie Delights' cash cycle suggesting that B should be chosen **Quality of product** It is important that customers feel that they are buying a quality product that reflects the brand. Supplier C's approach to stitching and materials may be seen as unacceptable, so could erode brand perception and loyalty, especially if this gets discussed on social media. Supplier B uses recyclable materials and so satisfies ethical concerns, whereas Supplier A is improving quality further by using double stitching. Unfortunately this may mean that the cost is too high resulting in Veggie Delights failing to hit the mark-up required. It is also debatable whether customers would value double stitching for a child's toy.

30 VEGGIE DELIGHTS' PLANNING

(a) Data table:

Quarter Number	Volume Units	Revenue £	Variable Cost £	Contribution £
1 (Q2 20X7)	350	8750	3500	5250
2 (Q3 20X7)	290	7250	2900	4350
3 (Q4 20X7)	266	6650	2660	3990
4 (Q1 20X8)	258	6450	2580	3870
5 (Q2 20X8)	246	6150	2460	3690
6 (Q3 20X8)	238	5950	2380	3570
7 (Q4 20X8)	205	5125	2050	3075
8 (Q1 20X9)	185	4625	1850	2775
9 (Q2 20X9)	165	4125	1650	2475
10 (Q3 20X9)	145	3625	1450	2175

Working: cost per meal = 25 × 0.40 = £10.00

*[Note: the first 6 quarters are **actual** results so will not fit the regression line exactly.]*

(b) Discussion of findings:

The value 'b'

The value b is the slope of the regression line, indicating by how much the value y declines (in this case) and the x value increases by 1 (1 quarter in this case). Hence it shows that sales volume is expected to decline by 20 meals per quarter as time ticks by. This is based on the average of past declines and there is no guarantee that past trend reflects the future. The decline could be greater or lower than the 20 meals given.

Data findings

The data shows that this product's revenue will fall to £3,625 by the end of the planning horizon (Q3 20X9). Over the same period the contribution gained also gradually falls and reaches only £2,175 by that same point.

The important point is that Veggie Delights will continue to make a positive contribution up to that quarter and so should be willing to continue to supply the product.

The data also states that this product's share of fixed costs are £2,500 and this might imply to some that cessation of supply is justified as the meal will be loss making. However, it must be borne in mind that these fixed costs will not be avoidable on cessation and as such are not relevant to a cessation decision. If they were directly attributable, then they would be relevant.

Furthermore, the data only relates to sales of that meal and does not include sales of new meals that might replace it on the menu.

(c) Non-financial considerations (2 needed)

Businesses should not make all decisions purely based on the financial figures and this case is no different. The following considerations are worthy of note:

Impact on customers – some customers may regard the signature dish as a trusted choice and may be disappointed if it is dropped

Impact on staff – presumably some staff were involved in perfecting the original dish and may get a strong sense of pride making it. They may thus feel aggrieved if it were dropped

Nature of decision – the decision is not set in stone – for example, the dish could still be offered on special occasions such as anniversaries

TASK 1.5

AO5	Analyse an organisation's decision making and control using ratio analysis.

31 OVERTRADING

(a) Complete the scorecard by calculating the missing ratios. (10 marks)

VEGGIE DELIGHTS Scorecard	**20Y0**	**20X9**
Profitability and gearing		
Gross profit %	46.5%	48.8%
Operating profit %	6.6%	**7.8%**
Return on capital employed	78.8%	**116.6%**
Gearing (debt/equity)	0.35×	0.04×
Liquidity ratios		
Current ratio	1.78:1	1.08:1
Acid test/Quick ratio	1.46:1	**0.98:1**
Working capital days		
Inventory holding period	4 days	**6 days**
Trade receivables collection period	3 days	0 days
Trade payables payment period	48 days	52 days
Working capital cycle	(41) days	**(46) days**

Workings

- Operating profit margin = (326,747/4,189,380) × 100% = 7.8%
- ROCE = [326,747/(9,675 + 270,443) × 100% = 116.6%
- Quick ratio = (1,073+354,888)/ 364,974= 0.98:1
- Inventory days = (36,947/2,146,134) × 365 = 6 days
- Working capital cycle = 6 + 0 - 52 = (46) days

(b) Select the ONE correct observation about each aspect of business performance below. **(10 marks)**

Profitability

20Y0 will be a year of steady, if unspectacular, progress. Although margins have dipped, the return on capital employed has been kept constant.	
The changes in gross margin could be due to cost control problems concerning distribution.	
Increased competition and the resulting pressure on prices could explain the change in each of the three profitability ratios.	✓

Gearing

The increased gearing ratio proves that the company has no problems raising additional debt finance.	
It is likely that the interest cover ratio has increased.	
The increased gearing ratio shows that the shareholders' position has become more risky.	✓

Liquidity

Both ratios have increased, which indicates that the company is less solvent.	
A higher quick ratio is a clear indicator of overtrading.	
The change in both the current and quick ratios could be partly explained by the increase in the receivables period.	✓

Working capital

The working capital cycle has worsened. This increases the possibility of Veggie Delights overtrading.	✓
There is a welcome improvement in the working capital cycle, mainly due to the change in the payment period for payables.	
The working capital cycle is worse than a year ago because of the change in inventory days.	

Overall performance

Despite overall growth, Veggie Delights is having a difficult year in 20Y0 and needs to investigate why key ratios are deteriorating.	✓
20Y0 looks to be a disaster for Veggie Delights.	
There is no evidence of possible control problems.	

32 COMPETITOR ANALYSIS

(a) Complete the scorecard by calculating the missing ratios. **(10 marks)**

20X9	**Veggie Delights**	**Rival**
Profitability		
Gross profit %	48.8%	**49.3%**
Operating profit %	7.8%	9.5%
Return on capital employed	116.6%	**27.9%**
Liquidity ratios		
Current ratio	1.1:1	**2.0:1**
Acid test/Quick ratio	1.0:1	0.6:1
Working capital days		
Inventory holding period	6 days	60 days
Trade receivables collection period	0 days	32 days
Trade payables payment period	52 days	**30 days**
Working capital cycle	(46) days	**62 days**

(b) Assess the following statements and indicate whether they are true or false.

(10 marks)

Statement	*True*	*False*
The difference in gross margins could be explained by the Rival giving vouchers in promotions to increase customer numbers in its restaurants.		✓
If Veggie Delights has delayed paying suppliers at the year end, then this would contribute to the difference in current ratios.	✓	
The difference in the lengths of the working capital cycles is more likely to be due to the rival's farming activities than its restaurants.	✓	
A restaurant employee in Veggie Delights was found to have stolen bar snacks and given them to friends. This would contribute to the difference in the ROCE figures.		✓
Inadequate controls over expense claims for managers within Veggie Delights could contribute to the difference in the operating margins figures.	✓	

33 CASH AND PROFIT

Why is profit important in business? (5 marks)

Profits are the generally accepted measure of the successful trading of a business.

Profit is the most commonly used measure of performance with analysts looking at figures for profit, profit margins and return on capital employed. As such the determination of profit is heavily regulated.

This regulation (in the form of standard accounting practices) ensures that all companies measure profit is broadly the same way and in this way, it is trusted by investors (such as the venture capitalists) and management to reflect performance.

The press often focusses on profitability when commenting on a business's performance and this tends to increase the profile of the profit measure on all concerned.

Why must cash also be considered in business? (5 marks)

Cash in this context is the cash balance of the business at any one time and also the amount of cash the business has generated or spent over the accounting period.

Cash is seen as vital in business for a number of reasons:

Cash is used for investment. If a business wants to buy assets in order to grow, then it needs cash to do that. It can borrow that money, that is true, but in this case it will need cash to make the repayments on any loan it takes out.

Cash is also used to make normal commercial payments. Wages, suppliers, and rent, all must be paid for with cash and so without cash these payments cannot be made and trade would stop.

The government also have a stake in businesses and although the regulation insists that profits are measured the government requires that corporate tax is paid. Although the amount of tax is in part determined by the profits made the company needs cash to actually make the payment.

Cash might also be needed for emergencies, to cover for example unexpected payments. Businesses often hold reserves of cash for this purpose.

Does the cash equal the profit? (5 marks)

In some ways, what Sean says is true. If he buys food or drink from a supplier then that will have to be paid for with cash. However, one important difference here is the timing of the purchase compared to the payment. There is often a lag between the purchase and the subsequent payment. Consequently although the two figures are the same they will be recorded at different points of time.

Also, there are other cash transactions that are not reflected in the profits of the business immediately. For example, when a business buys a new oven the cash outflow would be immediate and in total. The expense in the profit and loss account would slowly catch up over a number of years as depreciation is charged over the assets useful economic life but there would be a significant delay in the case of long existing assets.

The final major difference created between cash and profits is dividend. Dividend is a cash outflow but does not go through the profit and loss account at all.

For all the above reasons the amount a business has in cash is not equal to the profitability of the same business. In extreme cases, companies can be guilty of 'over-trading' – trying to grow too quickly and run out of cash despite being profitable.

Discuss whether delaying the rent payments will be effective in increasing profits and the ethical stance the accounting department should take to the request. (5 marks)

The accounts of a business are produced using generally accepted accounting principles. One of these is matching. The principle is that over an accounting period expense are related to that period regardless of the cash transactions.

What this means is that if a rent payment is delayed (as is being suggested in this case) then it would still be necessary to reflect the full rent cost in the profit and loss account and an accrual entry would be made to record it.

Consequently, delaying the rent payment would not be effective in increasing profits.

Ethically the accounts staff will be bound by an ethical code and would therefore be expected to behave professionally and with due care. Where it is being suggested that an accounting error (i.e. not posting the rent to boost profit) be deliberately made in order to manipulate the accounts then the accountants would have to resist and in some way refuse to make the adjustment.

TASK 1.6

Assessment objective 6	Analyse the internal controls of an organisation and make recommendations.

34 VEGGIE DELIGHTS' PAYROLL SYSTEMS

Identify and explain FIVE DEFICIENCIES in Veggie Delights' payroll system, and provide a recommendation to address each of these deficiencies. (15 marks)

Deficiency	Recommendation
Employees are not given a contract of employment. Staff could be under or over paid, or not work their contracted hours. This could result in disputes over terms of employment, leading to compensation being paid, or costs involved in employment tribunals.	All staff should be given a contract of employment which they are required to sign before commencing work. Existing staff should also be given a new contract as soon as possible.
The time recording machine is not in view and the clocking in/out process is not supervised. This could result in staff clocking in or out for their colleagues and the company paying for hours that have not been worked. This will increase payroll costs and cash outflows of the company.	The time recording machine should be relocated to where it is in view by other staff and the restaurant manager. The clocking in and out process should be supervised by the restaurant manager. Alternatively, another CCTV camera could be installed to record the clocking in and out process.

Deficiency	**Recommendation**
Spare clock cards are kept in the rack with the cards being used by staff. Staff could use the spare cards to create a duplicate wage claim. This will increase payroll costs and cash outflows of the company.	Spare clock cards should be kept locked away from the time recording machine. Staff should request a new one if theirs becomes damaged. The Payroll Manager, Nelson Badar, should regularly reconcile the number of active clock cards to the number of current staff, or perform a one to one check of named employees on cards, to staff records.
Employees take time to have a meal or drink once they have clocked in. Employees may take excessive meal breaks resulting in the company paying for time not worked. This will increase costs and cash outflows.	If the provision of meals is to continue, staff should be requested not to clock on until after they have finished their meal. The hours worked can be increased by a specified meal break time allowance e.g. 20 minutes.
The weekly clock cards are sent for processing with no checks or authorisation being undertaken. If staff have been fraudulently recording hours worked, this will not be picked up before the payments are made, unless by the Payroll Manager, Nelson Badar. This will increase costs and cash outflows for the company.	Before being sent off, the individual restaurant managers should review the clock cards for accuracy and sign to approve the hours worked. Before authorising payment, the Payroll Manager, Nelson Badar, should review the hours worked for reasonableness and investigate any significant discrepancies.
No records are retained of the gratuities earned by staff. This additional income may be taxable. The company may be liable for fines and penalties if they do not disclose this to the tax authorities on their employee's behalf.	The calculations of the gratuities should be recorded every month by the restaurant manager and passed to the Payroll Manager, Nelson Badar. Nelson should then include the details and consequences in the payroll calculations. **[1 mark]**

Note: only FIVE required

35 DALE FARM SALES AND DESPATCH SYSTEM

Identify and explain FIVE deficiencies in Dale Farm's sales and despatch system and provide a recommendation to address each of these deficiencies. (15 marks)

Deficiency	Recommendation
Inventory availability for telephone orders is not checked at the time the order is placed. The order clerks manually check the availability later and only then inform customers if there is insufficient inventory available. There is the risk that where goods are not available, order clerks could forget to contact the customers, leading to unfulfilled orders. This could lead to customer dissatisfaction, and would impact the farm's reputation.	When telephone orders are placed, the order clerk should check the inventory system whilst the customer is on the phone; they can then give an accurate assessment of the availability of goods and there is no risk of forgetting to inform customers.
Telephone orders are not recorded immediately on the three part pre-printed order forms; these are completed after the telephone call. There is a risk that incorrect or insufficient details may be recorded by the clerk and this could result in incorrect orders being despatched or orders failing to be despatched at all, resulting in a loss of customer goodwill.	All telephone orders should be recorded immediately on the three part pre-printed order forms. The clerk should also double check all the details taken with the customer over the telephone to ensure the accuracy of the order recorded.
Telephone orders are not sequentially numbered. Therefore if orders are misplaced whilst in transit to the despatch department, these orders will not be fulfilled, resulting in dissatisfied customers.	The three part pre-printed orders forms should be sequentially numbered and on a regular basis the despatch department should run a sequence check of orders received. Where there are gaps in the sequence, they should be investigated to identify any missing orders.
Customers are able to place online orders which will exceed their agreed credit limit by 10%. This increases the risk of accepting orders from bad credit risks.	Customer credit limits should be reviewed more regularly by a responsible official and should reflect the current spending pattern of customers. If some customers have increased the level of their purchases and are making payments on time, then these customers' credit limits could be increased. The online ordering system should be amended to not allow any orders to be processed which will exceed the customer's credit limit.

Deficiency	**Recommendation**
A daily pick list is used by the despatch department when sending out customer orders. However, it does not appear that the goods are checked back to the original order; this could result in incorrect goods being sent out.	In addition to the pick list, copies of all the related orders should be printed on a daily basis. When the goods have been picked ready to be despatched, they should be cross checked back to the original order. They should check correct quantities and product descriptions, as well as checking the quality of goods being despatched to ensure they are not damaged.
Additional staff have been drafted in to help the two sales clerks produce the sales invoices. As the extra staff will not be as experienced as the sales clerks, there is an increased risk of mistakes being made in the sales invoices. This could result in customers being under or overcharged.	Only the sales clerks should be able to raise sales invoices. As the farm is expanding, consideration should be given to recruiting and training more permanent sales clerks who can produce sales invoices.
Discounts given to customers are manually entered onto the sales invoices by sales clerks. This could result in unauthorised sales discounts being given as there does not seem to be any authorisation required. In addition, a clerk could forget to manually enter the discount or enter an incorrect level of discount for a customer, leading to the sales invoice being overstated and a loss of customer goodwill.	For customers who are due to receive a discount, the authorised discount levels should be updated to the customer master file. When the sales invoices for these customers are raised, their discounts should automatically appear on the invoice. The invoicing system should be amended to prevent sales clerks from being able to manually enter sales discounts onto invoices.

Note: only FIVE required

36 VEGGIE DELIGHTS' GENERAL LEDGER SYSTEM

Weakness	Suggestion for improvement
There appears to be no approval required for any journal entries made by Amar (or for that matter Lauren). This means that errors made in journals are much less likely to be discovered before the entry is made.	Journal suggestions should be formally drafted with reasons for them and approval sought. This approval should be indicated by a signature and the journal documentation filed.
Access to the general ledger is given to under-qualified staff. Lauren is the HR director making it unlikely that she holds an accounting qualification. Specifically, it is unlikely that the change to the rules for non-current assets could made correctly by someone without a thorough grasp of accounting rules. Errors could be made, deliberate or otherwise, in a crucial accounting document.	Access to the general ledger should be restricted to Agnes and Amar only and this access should require password entry. Passwords should be a secret, changed regularly and sufficiently complicated to prevent guesswork being successful.
General ledger accounts can be created without authorisation. Dubious transactions could be hidden more easily in accounts created for the purpose.	The creation of general ledger accounts should only be possible by either Agnes or Amar. In all cases when a general ledger account is created then the system should alert both Agnes and Amar that this has happened.
A change to accounting policy has been made without approval or indeed consultation. Accounting policies must be consistently applied and appropriate for the business. If changed then adjustments may be required in comparative figures and an explanation made in the financial statements	The board must approve changes to the accounting policy. Evidence for the need of such a change must be shown and the financial effect calculated.
The friendship between Agnes and Amar could undermine the controls within the business. There is evidence of this already as Agnes is not asking for sight of journals from Amar due to a "trusting" environment that exists between them.	The business would struggle to enforce a more business-like relationship at this stage (the friendship having been formed), consequently a third person should review all journals and jointly produced work. This might have to be an internal auditor or other person with the requisite accounting knowledge.

Section 4

MOCK ASSESSMENT QUESTIONS

TASK 1 **(20 marks)**

(a) At the end of each shift, restaurant managers are expected to count the cash in their tills, adjust for the initial float and reconciles this figure to the record of sales made from the till system that sitting.

Which of the following activities would be revealed by such a control? One mark for each correct answer. **(4 marks)**

A customer had used a promotional voucher to buy a discounted meal	Yes/No
A customer had added a tip into the cash they paid and the till operator forgot to separate this out and place it in the tips jar	Yes/No
A stolen credit card had been used by a customer	Yes/No
A member of staff had borrowed some cash, intending to return it later	Yes/No

(b) **Who has the statutory duty to prepare accounts for Veggie Delights?** **(2 marks)**

The company auditors.	
The directors of the company.	
Amar Hameer, the Financial Controller.	
Companies House.	

(c) Supul Khayyam, Accounts Payable Clerk, has asked you to show whether the following errors would be detected by reconciling the accounts payable ledger to the accounts payable control account.

Tick whether the errors shown would be detected or not **(5 marks)**

	Yes	No
A pricing error was spotted in a purchase invoice		
The wrong percentage quantity discount was calculated on an invoice		
A purchase invoice was debited to the supplier's account		
A purchase invoice was posted to the wrong supplier account		
VAT on a purchase invoice was posted to sundry expenses instead of the VAT control a/c.		

(d) Entry to the receivables ledger is protected by a password.

Which of the following passwords is the most secure? **(2 marks)**

Creditors365	
Veganburger	
246810	
KlerK7&%1	

(e) One of your roles within Veggie Delights is to help choose suitable suppliers. Evan Crabb, the owner of Crabb Farms has written you an email encouraging you to choose them as a supplier. Included in the email is the following sentence:

"I seem to have some spare tickets to the upcoming rugby international match and wondered if you would like to have them, as I gather that you are a rugby fan." **(4 marks)**

Which of the fundamental principles of ethical behaviour does this most threaten?

Confidentiality	
Objectivity	
Professional competence and due care	

What action should be taken?

You can accept but must advise the auditors	
You can accept but must advise your manager	
You must decline	

(f) **Which THREE of the following internal control procedures would be most effective for Veggie Delights in reducing the risk of fraud by restaurant staff?** **(3 marks)**

For each till, restaurant managers reconcile cash to recorded sales receipts.	
Staff have their bags searched when entering and leaving the premises	
All staff have to undergo criminal records checks before being employed	
CCTV cameras watch over all tills.	
The Finance Director monitors gross profit margins for each restaurant	

TASK 2 **(15 marks)**

The board of Veggie Delights are negotiating the purchase of Sanderfords Ltd, a producer of organic fruit juices and smoothies. As part of the process you have been asked to review Sanderfords' budgetary procedures.

Sanderfords undertakes long-term planning and 20X9 was year four of this five-year plan. To date, all four years' budgets are exactly as per the five-year plan, and none has been flexed for changes in activity.

You have been given access to the following variance report for 20X9 and accompanying commentary from the Operations Director:

Operating statement for year ended 31 December 20X9	**Budget**	**Actual**	**Variance**
Sales volume (bottles)	75,600	63,000	12,600
	£	£	£
Turnover	45,360	44,100	(1,260)
Variable costs:			
Direct materials	9,072	8,190	882
Direct labour	7,560	5,680	1,880
Variable overheads	6,048	6,290	(242)
Fixed costs:			
Production, administration, selling and distribution	2,276	2,445	(169)
Total costs	24,956	22,605	2,351
Operating profit	20,404	21,495	1,091

Commentary from Sanderfords Ltd's Operations Director regarding the past financial year

Sales volume fell short of the budget by 17%, compared to a 15% shortfall last year. Our range of innovative products continues to be well-received by the market and we have won many awards, so it is disappointing that sales targets have not been met. We put up prices to support our high quality brand and imposed a new system of sales targets for staff but the growth has yet to materialise.

There were, however, some significant cost savings, so overall profit exceeded budget.

Direct materials was less than budget, reflecting good cost control in the factory.

During 20X8, the company experienced some difficulty in employing enough labour to pick fruit and work in the processing factory, so at the end of 20X8 we incorporated more automation, resulting labour cost savings in 20X9, albeit at the expense of higher overheads.

Selling and distributions costs were well-controlled.

Unfortunately other fixed costs increased but we are not sure why.

(a) **Evaluate and make recommendations for improving Sanderfords' approach to planning and budgetary control.** **(8 marks)**

(b) **Evaluate the Operations Director's explanations of the variances, giving revised variances where appropriate.** **(7 marks)**

(Total: 15 marks)

(a) Planning and Budgetary Control **(8 marks)**

(b) Variances **(7 marks)**

TASK 3 **(15 marks)**

Extract of purchases and payables system

Restaurant managers are responsible for ordering drinks and food for their restaurants. Each week a restaurant manager will raise a purchase requisition form, which is sent to the Purchasing Manager, Lokesh Ashtari. Lokesh consolidates the orders, chooses suppliers and places the orders. He sends any individual orders above £1,000 for authorisation from the Finance Director. A copy of the resulting purchase order for each restaurant is then emailed to each restaurant manager.

Receipts of goods from suppliers are processed by staff at each restaurant, depending on who is free at the time. Ideally the purchase order has been printed off by the restaurant manager, so the member of staff can check quantity and quality of goods against it. Unfortunately this does not always happen. What does happen is that members of staff will complete a sequentially numbered blank goods received note (GRN). The GRNs are sent to the accounts department every two weeks for processing.

On receipt of the purchase invoice from the supplier, an accounts clerk matches it to the GRN. The invoice is then sent to the Purchasing Manager, Lokesh Ashtari, who processes it for payment. The Finance Director is given the total amount of the payments list, which she authorises and then processes the bank payments. Due to staff shortages in the accounts department, supplier statement reconciliations are no longer performed.

Use the answer spaces overleaf as follows:

- **Identify and explain five weaknesses from the above system description**
- **For each weakness briefly explain the effect it could have on the company**

Weakness	Effect of Weakness

TASK 4 **(15 marks)**

Due to increased competition from new rivals, the Board of Veggie Delights are considering closing one existing restaurant in the small village of Winkton, just outside of Christchurch.

Sergey Dashdamirov, Regional Operations Manager, has produced the following schedule of costs and benefits of the closure but you have been asked to consider the approach and report back.

Item	Notes	Impact of closure
Research costs	Cost incurred to date in researching the different options concerning closure. This has cost £3,000 to date including director's time.	Cost of £3,000
Rent and rates	The existing restaurant is rented for £96,000 per annum. The lease comes to an end shortly and Veggie Delights will be able to exit. This rent will thus be saved.	Saving of £96,000
Wages	While some existing Veggie Delights staff will be able to get jobs being advertised in other existing restaurants, most will have to be made redundant or take early retirement. Staff costs for the next year were expected to be £120,000.	Saving of £120,000
Profit or loss on operations	The restaurant made an operating profit of £52,000 in 20X9 but is expected to make a loss of £25,000 over the next twelve months. This loss will be avoided by closure.	Saving of £25,000
Equipment	The old kitchen equipment – ovens, fridges, pans, etc – will be sold. The equipment currently has a net book value of £16,000 and will be sold for an estimated £10,000. There will thus be a loss on disposal of £6,000.	Loss of £6,000

You have been asked to review this analysis using the principles of relevant costing to help ensure that the correct decision is made.

Use the answer spaces overleaf as follows:

- **Briefly explain the principles behind relevant cash flows for decision making. (3 marks)**
- **Comment on each of the costs above as to whether the figures given for the impact are correct. (12 marks)**

(Total: 15 marks)

Relevant cash flow principles

Item	**Comment on treatment**
Research costs	
Loss avoided	
Rent saved	

Item	**Comment on treatment**
Staff costs avoided	
Equipment loss on disposal	

TASK 5 **(20 marks)**

Veggie Delights is considering opening some new restaurants as franchises.

Under such a scheme the roles of the franchisee and the franchisor (i.e. Veggie Delights) would be as follows:

- Veggie Delights would acquire the premises. The franchisee then fits them out with kitchen equipment and fixtures and fittings.
- The franchisee would pay Veggie Delights an initial lump sum for the right to use the Veggie Delights name and run the franchise
- Veggie Delights would supply all staff training and marketing, including the website operations
- The franchisee would have control over day to day operations but would be subject to various quality control measures imposed by Veggie Delights, such as only offering meat-free meals, having to use approved suppliers, etc.
- The franchisee would pay Veggie Delights an annual fixed fee plus 5% of its revenue

To help assess franchising as a vehicle for expansion, Conor Seddon, Commercial Manager, has obtained the following financial statements for a franchised fast food restaurant:

Extracts from accounts of franchised fast food restaurant	**20X9 £000**
Profitability	
Sales revenue	3,945
Cost of sales	(2,070)
Gross profit	1,875
Payments to franchisor	(225)
Other operating costs	(1,413)
Profit from operations	**237**
Assets	
Non-current assets	214
Inventories	113
Trade receivables	15
Cash	380
Total	**722**
Equities and liabilities	
Equity	300
Non-current liabilities – loans	0
Trade payables	397
Tax liabilities	25
Total	**722**

(a) Complete the scorecard by calculating the missing ratios. (10 marks)

20X9	**Veggie Delights**	**Franchise**
Profitability		
Gross profit %	48.8%	
Operating profit %	7.8%	6.0%
Liquidity ratios		
Current ratio	1.1:1	
Acid test/Quick ratio	1.0:1	0.9:1
Working capital days		
Inventory holding period	6 days	
Trade receivables collection period	0 days	1 day
Trade payables payment period	52 days	
Working capital cycle	(46) days	

(b) Assess the following statements and indicate whether they are true or false. (10 marks)

Statement	*True*	*False*
The difference in gross margins could be explained by the Franchisee having to abide by tougher food quality standards than Veggie Delights.		
The difference in operating margins could be explained by the Franchisee not having to pay for marketing costs.		
The difference in quick ratios can be explained by the Franchisee not owning their building.		
The difference in inventory holding periods could be explained by Veggie Delights being less willing to use frozen ingredients in its meals.		
The Franchisee in this case typically receives money from customers before it has to pay suppliers.		

TASK 6 **(15 marks)**

Veggie Delights' cash receipts system

You have been asked to review theinternal controls of Veggie Delights in relation to the cash receipts system.

Each of Veggie Delights' restaurants has on average three or four cash tills to take customer payments. All employees based at the store are able to use each till and individuals do not have their own log on codes, although employees tend to use the same till each day. Customers can pay using either cash or a credit card and for any transaction either the credit card payment slips or cash are placed in the till by the cashier. Where employees' friends or family members purchase food or drink in the restaurant, the employee is able to serve them at the till point.

At the end of each day, the tills are closed down with daily readings of sales taken from each till. These are reconciled to the total of the cash in the tills and the credit card payment slips and any discrepancies are noted. To save time, this reconciliation is done by the restaurant manager in aggregate for all of the restaurant tills together. Once this reconciliation has taken place, the cash is stored in the restaurant's small safe overnight and in the morning it is transferred to the bank via collection by a security company. If the restaurant is low on change for cash payments, a junior member of staff is sent by a till operator to the bank with money from the till and asked to change it into smaller denominations.

The daily sales readings from the tills along with the cash data and credit card payment data are transferred daily to head office through an interface with the sales and cash receipts records. The cashier, Tommy Mills, oversees that this transfer has occurred for all stores. On a daily basis, he also agrees the cash transferred by the security company has been banked in full by agreeing the cash deposit slips to the bank statements, and that the credit card receipts have been received from the credit card company. On a monthly basis, the same clerk reconciles the bank statements to the cash book. The reconciliations are reviewed by the financial controller, Amar Hameer, if there are any unreconciled amounts.

Required:

In respect of the cash receipts system of Veggie Delights, identify and explain FIVE deficiencies and recommend a control to address each of these deficiencies.

Deficiencies	Controls

Deficiencies	Controls

Section 5

ANSWERS TO MOCK ASSESSMENT QUESTIONS

TASK 1

(a) Which of the following activities would be revealed by such a control? (4 marks)

A customer had used a promotional voucher to buy a discounted meal	No
A customer had added a tip into the cash they paid and the till operator forgot to separate this out	Yes
A stolen credit card had been used by a customer	No
A member of staff had borrowed some cash, intending to return it later	Yes

(b) Who has the statutory duty to prepare accounts for Veggie Delights? (2 marks)

The company auditors.	
The directors of the company.	✓
Amar Hameer, the Financial Controller.	
Companies House.	

(c) Tick whether the errors shown would be detected or not (5 marks)

	Yes	No	Explanation
A pricing error was spotted in a purchase invoice		✓	*Wrong figure posted to both so still agree*
The wrong percentage quantity discount was calculated on an invoice		✓	*Wrong figure posted to both so still agree*
A purchase invoice was debited to the supplier's account	✓		*Only accounts payable ledger wrong*
A purchase invoice was posted to the wrong supplier account		✓	*Both totals still correct, so agree*
VAT on a purchase invoice was posted to sundry expenses instead of the VAT control a/c.		✓	*Neither affected*

(d) Which of the following passwords is the most secure? **(2 marks)**

Creditors365	
Veganburger	
246810	
KlerK7&%1	✓

Generally, the more complicated the better, avoiding words, names and strings of any sort.

(e) Which of the fundamental principles of ethical behaviour does this most threaten?

Confidentiality	
Objectivity	✓
Professional competence and due care	

What action should be taken?

You can accept but must advise the auditors	
You can accept but must advise your manager	
You must decline	✓

(f) Which THREE of the following internal control procedures would be most effective for Veggie Delights in reducing the risk of fraud by restaurant staff? **(3 marks)**

For each till, restaurant managers reconcile cash to recorded sales receipts.	✓
Staff have their bags searched when entering and leaving the premises	✓
All staff have to undergo criminal records checks before being employed	
CCTV cameras watch over all tills.	✓
The Finance Director monitors gross profit margins for each restaurant	

TASK 2

(a) **Planning**

Strengths

- Company undertakes long term planning
- Length of the plan (5 years) is realistic and is in line with typical commercial practices

Weaknesses

- Long term plan is fixed – has not been changed to reflect falls in sales volume, price rises or increased automation.
- Fixed plan has led to the sales volume budget for 20X9 being unrealistic
- Targets are imposed on managers, potentially resulting in unrealistic targets and demotivated managers

Recommendations

- A rolling 5-year plan would be better (particularly when major changes occur). This would mean that at end of each year, a new 5th year plan would be added in and so should reflect changes in the business environment, such as competition.
- Greater participation in target setting would increase motivation, albeit at the risk of padding.

Budgetary control

Strengths

- Company is using variance analysis - Variance analysis involves comparing budgeted and actual costs and revenues to produce the differences (variances).
- Should enable "management by exception", facilitating more effective control and use of management time

Weaknesses

- Variances are meaningless in this situation as they are produced against fixed budget. Obviously one would expect costs to be lower as sales volume is 17% lower than expected.
- Variances do not appear to be investigated – the Operations Director does not seem to know why a large cost overrun has occurred.
- Variances are only considered in total and not broken down into sub-variances. For example, it would be useful to break labour variances down into rate and usage factors.

Recommendations

- Budgets should be flexed for a more valid comparison
- Variances should be broken down into sub-variances to help identify causes
- Significant variances should be investigated

(b) **Variances**

The Operations Director's comments are limited by the fact that the budget has not been flexed.

Sales variances

- A flexed sales budget would give 45,360 × 63,000/75,600 = 37,800
- This would give a favourable sales price variance of £6,300
- The Director stated that prices had been put up but, without further information, it is unclear how this variance compares

Direct materials

- A flexed materials budget would give 9,072 × 63,000/75,600 = 7,560
- This would give an adverse materials variance of £630
- The director commented that there was good cost control in the factory, but an adverse variance indicates the opposite – either more ingredients are being used/wasted and/or prices have increased. It is vital that this is investigated.

Direct labour

- A flexed materials budget would give 7,560 × 63,000/75,600 = 6,300
- This would give a smaller favourable labour variance of £620
- The director commented that additional automation had been incorporated at the end of 20X8, which would explain why less labour was required. However, it would be better to revise the standard cost card for labour and recalculate rate and efficiency variances to understand more deeply any control issues.

Variable overheads

- A flexed variable OH budget would give 6,048 × 63,000/75,600 = 5,040
- This would give a larger adverse variable OH variance of £1,290
- The director did state that automation may have increased overheads, which does make sense in terms of higher energy costs, say. However, the size of the variance means it should be prioritised.

Fixed overheads

- The fixed OH budget does not need flexing, so the variance shown is valid.
- The director did state that automation may have increased overheads, which does make sense in terms of higher depreciation, say.

TASK 3

Weakness and effect thereof:

Weakness	**Effect of Weakness**
Purchase orders below £1,000 are not authorised and are processed solely by the purchase order clerk who is also responsible for processing invoices.	This could result in non-business related purchases and there is an increased fraud risk as the clerk could place orders for personal goods up to the value of £1,000, which is significant.
Goods received notes (GRNs) are only sent to the accounts department every two weeks.	This could result in delays in suppliers being paid as the purchase invoices could not be agreed to a GRN and also recorded liabilities being understated. Additionally, any prompt payment discounts offered by suppliers may be missed due to delayed payments.
GRNs are only sent to the accounts department.	Failing to send a copy to the purchasing department could result in unfulfilled orders not being detected, leading to stock-outs and restaurants being unable to offer all the meals on their menu.
The the Purchasing Manager, Lokesh Ashtari, has responsibility for ordering goods below $1,000 and for processing all purchase invoices for payment.	There is a lack of segregation of duties and this increases the risk of fraud and non-business related purchases being made.
The finance director authorises the bank transfer payment list for suppliers; however, she only views the total amount of payments to be made.	Without looking at the detail of the payments list, as well as supporting documentation, there is a risk that suppliers could be being paid an incorrect amount, or that sums are being paid to fictitious suppliers.
Supplier statement reconciliations are no longer performed.	This may result in errors in the recording of purchases and payables not being identified in a timely manner.

TASK 4

Relevant cash flow principles

The principles behind the idea of relevant costing for decisions

When any decision is being made it can be difficult to determine exactly which figures should be incorporated and how significant they are. The principle behind relevant costing is that we only incorporate factors that are directly affected by the decision and to the extent that they are affected.

For an item to be included it should be:

- A future item: past costs and revenues are known as sunk and are ignored
- A cash flow: provisions, depreciations are not cash flow and should be excluded
- An incremental amount

  If, for example, we are comparing two possible outcomes:

Cash position if we go ahead with the proposal	£A
Cash position if we reject the proposal	£B

The relevant cash flow is the 'future incremental cash flow' and is the difference between the two outcomes = A – B

Comments of existing treatment:

Item	Comment on treatment
Research costs	These are sunk costs (past costs) and should be excluded from the appraisal.
Rent and rates	The rent for the old restaurant will indeed be saved from the date the lease ends. However, the schedule only includes one year's rent. A decision needs to be made how many years' worth of future costs and revenues should be included in the decision (not just for rent). Ideally discounted future cash flows should be used to determine the NPV of closure When leases end there can also sometimes be extra payments to return the property to its original condition. These are called dilapidations and are relevant costs that should also be included.
Wages	The staff that manage to get jobs advertised in other existing restaurants will get paid whether we close or not, so their salary is not relevant to the decision to move. Veggie Delights needs to compare the total wages before with the wages after the move to identify the relevant cash flow. Any redundancy costs that would be paid if closure takes place would also have to be included as relevant cash flows.
Profit or loss on operations	Operating profit will be calculated after deducting wages and rent, so Sergey's schedule is effectively double counting these items. It would be better to focus on each line in the profit and loss separately. In terms of items not covered in the above lines, the following points can be made:

	Predicted revenue will be lost, so this will give rise to a relevant cost. However, it may be that some customers will visit other Veggie Delights instead, so the incremental impact may not be as great. Similarly estimated food costs and energy costs will be avoided and the incremental saving included. Any head office costs apportioned the restaurant will not be saved by closure, so should be excluded. Note: instead of mentioning sales and materials costs separately, you have discussed the need to focus on contribution rather than profit
Equipment	The NBV is made up of the original purchase price, which is sunk, and accumulated depreciation to date. Depreciation is not a cash flow and should be excluded. What is relevant here is the net realisable (i.e. scrap) value of the old equipment – i.e. a £10,000 cash inflow

TASK 5

(a) Complete the scorecard by calculating the missing ratios. (10 marks)

20X9	**Veggie Delights**	**Franchise**
Profitability		
Gross profit %	48.8%	47.5%
Operating profit %	7.8%	6.0%
Liquidity ratios		
Current ratio	1.1:1	1.2:1
Acid test/Quick ratio	1.0:1	0.9:1
Working capital days		
Inventory holding period	6 days	20 days
Trade receivables collection period	0 days	1 day
Trade payables payment period	52 days	70 days
Working capital cycle	(46) days	(49) days

Gross profit %:	1,875/3,945	= 47.5%
Current ratio:	508/422	= 1.2:1
Inventory holding period:	(113/2,070) × 365	= 20 days
Trade payables period:	(397/2,070) × 365	= 75 days
Working capital cycle:	20 + 1 – 70	= (49) days

(b) Assess the following statements and indicate whether they are true or false. (10 marks)

Statement	*Note*	*True*	*False*
The difference in gross margins could be explained by the Franchisee having to abide by tougher food quality standards than Veggie Delights.	1	✓	
The difference in operating margins could be explained by the Franchisee not having to pay for marketing costs.	2		✓
The difference in quick ratios can be explained by the Franchisee not owning their building.	3		✓
The difference in inventory holding periods could be explained by Veggie Delights being less willing to use frozen ingredients in its meals.	4	✓	
The Franchisee in this case typically receives money from customers before it has to pay suppliers.	5	✓	

Notes:

1. If the franchisee has to abide by tougher food standards (presumably imposed by the Franchisor), then it will have higher food purchase and preparation costs, increasing its cost of sales and reducing its gross margin.
2. While it is true that the franchisee does not pay directly for marketing, this (viewed in isolation) would give it a higher operating margin rather than the lower one seen here. Furthermore, the statement is also false as the franchisee does effectively pay for marketing via the payment mechanism of annual fee plus a % of revenue.
3. Non-current assets do not feature in the quick ratio.
4. The company selected is a fast food restaurant so may well be more willing to use frozen ingredients. This would explain why the rival has a higher holding period.
5. A negative cash operating cycle does indicate that cash is received from customers before making payment to suppliers.

TASK 6

Deficiencies	Controls
All restaurant employees are able to use each till and none have an individual log on code when using the tills. Allowing all employees access to the till points increases the risk of fraud and error arising. Also in the event of cash discrepancies arising in the tills, it would be difficult to ascertain which employees may be responsible as there is no way of tracking who used which till.	Only employees for whom criminal record/credit checks have been undertaken should be able to use the tills to take customer payments. Each employee should have a designated till and a log on code, which is required for each payment transaction.
The daily reading of sales and reconciliations to the tills is performed in aggregate rather than for each till. This means if exceptions arise, it will be difficult to identify which till caused the difference and therefore which employees may require further till training or have undertaken fraudulent transactions.	The reconciliations should be undertaken on an individual till by till basis rather than in aggregate.
Where employees' friends or family members purchase food or drink in the restaurant, the employee is able to serve them at the till point. There is a significant fraud risk as employees could fail to put the items through the till, but retain the cash paid by the friend/family members. Additionally, they could give food or drink away for free or undercharge for items sold, thereby granting unauthorised discounts.	Veggie Delights should instigate a policy whereby employees are unable to serve friends or family members at the till points. They should be required to request that a manager or supervisor put these items through the till. In addition, CCTV cameras could be placed in the restaurants, near to the till points to record the daily till transactions. This would act as a deterrent to employees as well as provide evidence in the case of fraudulent transactions occurring. Also Veggie Delights should carry out regular inventory counts to identify if food and drink stocks in the restaurants are below the levels in the inventory records, as this could identify items being given away for free.
The cashing up of tills along with the recording of any cash discrepancies is undertaken by just one individual, the restaurant manager. There is a fraud risk as the restaurant manager could remove some of the cash and then simply record that there was an exception on this till.	The cashing up process should be undertaken by two individuals together, ideally the assistant and the store manager. One should count the cash and the other record it. Any exceptions to the till reading should be double checked to confirm that they are not simply addition errors.

The cash is kept at the restaurant overnight in a small safe. Although in a safe, this is not secure as it is likely that the cash sales for one day would be a significant sum. This cash is at risk of being stolen overnight.	The cash should continue to be collected daily by the security company, but rather than in the morning it should be collected as the store closes in the evening so that cash does not have to be stored overnight.
If a store needs change, a junior staff member is sent to the bank by a till operator to change it into smaller denominations. There is a risk of the cash being misplaced or stolen on the way to the bank or collusion between the junior staff member and till operator as no record appears to be kept of the money removed from the till in these instances and no confirmation of how much cash is returned is carried out.	Veggie Delights' head office should stipulate a float amount per till and how the note denominations should be comprised. When assigning the cash float in the morning, the restaurant manager should ensure that this policy is adhered to. If during the day, further smaller denomination notes are required, the restaurant manager should authorise a member of staff to obtain cash from the bank and should fully record movements in and out of the till.
One clerk is responsible for several elements of the cash receipts system. He oversees the daily interface from stores, agrees that cash has cleared into the bank statements and undertakes the bank reconciliations. There is a lack of segregation of duties and errors will not be identified on a timely basis as well as increasing the risk of fraud.	These key roles should be split between a few individuals, with ideally the bank reconciliations being undertaken by another member of the finance team.
The bank reconciliations are only reviewed by the financial controller if there are any unreconciled amounts. The bank reconciliation could reconcile but still contain significant errors as there could be compensating errors which cancel each other out. In addition, for a cash based business, the bank reconciliation is a key control which reduces the risk of fraud. If it is not reviewed, then this reduces its effectiveness.	The bank reconciliations should be reviewed by the financial controller on a monthly basis, even if there are no exceptions, and he should evidence his review by way of signature on the bank reconciliation.

Note: Only **FIVE** needed